# Will Jesus kick my ball back?

## Jennifer Minney

*Silvertree Publishing*

Published 2000
by
Silvertree Publishing
PO Box 2768, Yeovil, Somerset

ISBN: 0-9538446-0-9

This is a true story, and the events are historically accurate.
However the names of many of the characters have been altered.

A catalogue record for this book is available from the
British Library

Printed and bound by
Redwood Books, Trowbridge

## To Jonathan

I did not fashion you,
A seedling in a welcome womb,
Planted, planned in love;
But in an aching heart
Conceived you, formless, undefined,
With hope sprung from above.

I did not carry  you
For nine short months, enveloped soft
Within a watery nest;
But in my every thought
Upheld you, year by weary year,
With tears by heaven blessed.

I did not give you birth:
Expel you, squealing, naked, wet,
From pain-racked body rent;
But torn in soul — afraid
To lose you, full of wondrous joy —
I gave you life's intent.

I did not nurture you
With swollen breasts that softly flowed
With milk, sustaining, sweet;
But from my every pore
There streamed unending rich supplies
Of mother-love complete.

# Chapter 1

Brian was getting used to my mind being anywhere but where my body was. So when he asked me to marry him, and I gave him a vacant stare and said, "What!" he just grinned and repeated the question.

I had just come off-duty after a hectic day on the children's surgical ward, and my mind was still on one of my patients: a little boy with an impish face who had kept me laughing all the time I was changing his dressing. He was a lovely child, and I had wished I could take him home with me.

But now, as my thoughts focused on the man sprawled opposite, in the shabby old chair in my room at the nurses' home, the picture of the child, the dressing trolley and the ward instantly faded. And I grinned back at him.

The first time I met Brian, at a church social, he had been sitting on the floor; and as I watched sparkles of firelight flickering through his shoulder-length blond hair, the thought had come to me, I will be seeing that blond hair for a long time. I had known, from that moment, that I would marry him. And now I put my arms around his thick neck, laid my dark head against his blond one, and said a very definite, "Yes."

Suddenly, the thought struck me: now I can have children! I had always wanted four — two boys and two girls. And at the age of twenty-eight, with my biological clock ticking away, I could hardly wait to get started. But first we had to organise the wedding around nursing exams, and then I wanted to train as a midwife. So it would be nearly three years before I could begin to produce my dream family.

Part way through midwifery training I decided that I couldn't wait any longer. Brian and I had been married just over a year, and now that we were getting settled financially we were talking more than ever about starting a family. I often daydreamed about my babies; imagining being pregnant, giving birth, breast-feeding.... I pictured our children growing up, and Brian and I

5

playing with them, teaching them, having fun. I once asked him if he thought they would be blond like him or dark like me. "Striped," he had replied drily.

We now discussed the more practical issue of whether I could cope with final midwifery exams when I was six months pregnant. I decided that I could, and with a feeling of exhilaration threw away my contraceptives. That first month, I was in a constant state of excitement, wondering if I was pregnant. But I wasn't. And neither was I pregnant the next month — or the next — or the next. The final midwifery exams came and went. Another six months passed. And then, with a sense of failure and defeat, I went to the doctor's. And now began, not just a repeating cycle of hope, excitement and disappointment, but the painful and humiliating round of tests and operations.

My first operation was an exploratory one: a laparoscopy. And it was discovered that, due to a perforated appendix when I was four, all my pelvic organs were stuck together by a tangled mass of adhesions. The doctors suspected that my oviducts (Fallopian tubes) were partially blocked, and they confirmed this by injecting a radioactive dye and taking x-rays.

Afterwards, I lay in bed wondering why my shoulders were so painful. As a registered nurse and midwife, I knew that this was referred pain, due to pressure on the diaphragm, and I had been half expecting it But I hadn't thought it would be so bad. But the doctors were pleased about the pain, saying that it showed more dye had got through than the x-rays seemed to indicate. And I felt a surge of hope. The pain now seemed as nothing, especially when I discovered that I could shift it from one shoulder to the other by swinging my hips from side to side. And the next week I went back to work on the labour ward, convinced that within a year, I too would be giving birth.

Another six months passed. And still I wasn't pregnant. So this time the doctors tried insufflation: forcing air through the ducts. Until then I had always been very stoical: I could endure, and conceal, any amount of pain. But not on this occasion. For about an hour afterwards I lay face down on the theatre trolley, writhing with pain and biting on the pillow to stifle the escaping moans. Eventually, my blanket slipped off and fell to the floor, and I knew that my op gown was open all down the back, leaving my bare behind exposed to the world. But I was past caring. All I wanted was for someone to give me an injection and knock me into oblivion. And I vowed, never again.

I went back to work, and Brian and I started again trying to conceive. Although I was ovulating normally, already I was getting caught up in the hassle of thermometers and temperature charts. The baby thing was beginning to take over, although I tried very hard to think about other things. Brian and I were happily married, we'd had a lot of fun buying our first house and setting up home, and we had many shared interests: literature, art, music, as well as our Christian faith. And we'd had some wonderful weekends camping. And yet, as each month passed, each month seeming like a year, and I still wasn't pregnant, I could no longer blot out the picture of a child. It superimposed itself on everything.

Not only were we unable to conceive, we were also unable to adopt. We wrote to one adoption agency after another, and from every one we received the same pre-printed reply: due to the backlog of childless couples wanting the few available babies, their lists were closed. But we persisted. And at last we received a letter from a Christian agency, inviting us to go for an interview. We went, full of mingled hope and fear. After so many rejections, we felt that this was our last chance. The interview went well, but we were told that there was one thing against us: we hadn't been married long enough. "Come back when you've been married five years," said the interviewer. Then he added, "though by then, you'll probably be considered too old."

I was devastated, feeling that, since I could neither conceive nor adopt, there was nothing to look forward to. I could never be a mother, and neither could I concentrate on my career. Day after day I was bringing new babies into the world, witnessing the miracle of birth, seeing the look of joy and wonder on the parents' faces, sharing — and yet excluded from — those first moments of bonding. And every time, I felt such an agony of longing that it was becoming unbearable.

7

It wasn't much better on the antenatal or post-natal wards, and I began to dread having to go to work. Every day was a dark battle with feelings of envy and despair. But one in particular I would never forget. One of my patients was having regular contractions, and I was taking her down to the labour ward. She looked fearful and upset, and I tried to encourage her, reminding her that soon she would be holding a precious new baby in her arms. She turned on me angrily and said, "You ought to be glad you're not in my place."

"I would give everything I possess to be in your place," I told her quietly. And I meant it.

Of course I prayed — we both did. But while for Brian prayer was a calm request for something he desired but could live without, for me it was one long cry of anguish. Night and day I pleaded with God to give us a child. And one night he spoke to me. Unable to sleep, I was staggering around the living room, as usual sobbing out my incoherent petition, when I suddenly understood — really understood — why Eli had thought Hannah was drunk. She *was* drunk — drunk with the torment of her barrenness; in those Old Testament days, not only a cause of grief, but of shame and humiliation. My mind jumped from Hannah to Rachel, and from Rachel to Sarah. Then, in the midst of my torment, I clearly heard the words Sarah had spoken so long ago: "God has made me to laugh, and all who hear will laugh with me."

I didn't know if the words were audible, or if they came from somewhere deep inside me. But I knew for certain that I had not imagined them. They were so clear that they stopped me in my tracks. And as I stood there, wondering, a sense of peace stole over me. Then I started to laugh: not a hysterical outburst of grief, but an overflowing of relief and joy. And from that moment, although I never stopped experiencing the pain of childlessness, deep down I knew that, one day, I would have a child of my own.

But like Sarah, I couldn't wait. I wanted my child now. And with renewed hope, Brian and I began writing again to

8

adoption agencies and Social Services departments. At last, when we had been married three years, we were told that we could foster a two-year old boy with a view to adoption. He was one of twins — the only one to survive — who had been born prematurely, and he was brain damaged. Not only was he mentally retarded, he was also undersized and emotionally disturbed. He was so disturbed, in fact, that the first time we met him the social workers warned us not to approach him, but to wait for him to come to us. It might, they said, take several visits before he would come anywhere near us.

We saw at once what they meant. He was a scrawny little mite, with two thick yellow candles of mucus running from his nose, and he sat rocking himself in a corner, his arms across his face, and a look of terror in his big, brown eyes. In later years, we realised that he had been showing typical signs of child abuse; but then we naively thought that, since he'd been in a children's home all his life, he couldn't possibly have been abused. And we sat chatting to the social workers while he rocked in the corner, and all the time I was aching to go to him and pick him up — having first wiped his nose — thinking that all he needed was a bit of love and attention.

It did not take several visits for Mark to come to us. It took half an hour. The social workers were amazed, and sat there, staring in disbelief while he leaned against my knee, and then climbed onto it. He promptly "christened" me. And, as the urine soaked into my skirt, and I began jiggling Mark to one side, pulling my sodden clothes away from my legs, the tense silence exploded in laughter. The visit went so well that, the next time we saw Mark, we took him home with us.

And now we discovered just how fearful of people Mark really was. He cried if anyone came near him, rushing to a corner where he would sit, shaking and trembling. We couldn't take him into crowded places, and at first even church was too much for him. I often wondered why he had come to me at that first meeting. But then, people had often laughed at the way I attracted children and dogs. I had dreamed of having a house full of children and animals; a house full of noise and love and laughter. And here I was, with one, very disturbed, very

9

unsociable child who cried constantly, day and night, and who could be taken from us at any moment.

But we persevered with him. And eventually he lost his fear and became a happy, outgoing, very affectionate little boy. And he grew so much that we nicknamed him Topsy. The social workers often wondered if this was the same child, and I was delighted with their recognition of all the love and care we had invested in him. And I felt a great sense of achievement. But, I was also lonely and bored. I was missing the company of my work colleagues, the noise and bustle of the wards, the mental stimulation. I enjoyed being a mother, but it was not as fulfilling as I had imagined, and I wondered anxiously what was wrong with me, especially as I found myself sometimes getting angry with Mark, often for no apparent reason.

In time, I began to realise that, much as I loved Mark, I had been angry from the first moments, when I saw him cowering in a corner, because that was me as a child. I had grown up with fear, terrified of my sadistically violent father and unpredictable, explosive mother, and I didn't want to be reminded of that. Later, I had become angry and impatient with his slow-ness, his clumsiness, his being less than perfect. But perhaps most of all, I was angry because he wasn't mine, because I had to live with the fear of losing him.

In spite of having been abused, mentally and physically, by both parents for nineteen years, and having lived constantly with the fear of rejection and expulsion, I had thought that merely becoming a Christian would wipe out all the pain, and associated anger, of the past. And even now, years later, I still hadn't fully grasped that becoming a Christian was just the beginning: the beginning of a journey of discovery of God's love and acceptance, and the healing that comes through being loved and accepted. I had come a long way in my Christian journey, but not far enough. The truth was, Mark had opened up old wounds — wounds that had never truly healed. And until they healed, I was not ready for a child; certainly not a damaged, retarded child who demanded so very much.

Deep in my soul, I knew this truth. But I would not —

could not — accept it. So, when Mark had been with us a year and we were told that we could begin adoption proceedings, we went ahead. The whole thing was a nightmare: the endless forms to fill in, the group meetings, interviews, medicals, police checks.... I started to feel like a criminal. And it seemed so unfair that other couples could decide they wanted a baby, go ahead and conceive one, and that was that, while I had to be inspected and scrutinised and judged.

And then, late one Friday, our social worker phoned to say that they had received a call from the new leader of Mark's play-group, where he went every morning. She was concerned about recurring bruises on his shins, just below his knees. The social worker asked if I knew what had caused them, and I said that I didn't, adding that Brian and I had noticed them and been puzzled by them. She told me not to worry, saying, "We get reports of abuse all the time, and most of them are groundless."

Then she told me to take Mark to the doctor's on Monday morning and get him checked out, just so they could clear their records. She was very matter-of-fact about it, but I was stunned and bewildered, and very frightened. My head felt very fuzzy as I tried to take it in, and I couldn't think clearly — the doctor's — there was some reason why I couldn't go to the doctor's. I started to tell her there was something — then I remembered. We had an appointment with Mark at the hospital eye clinic. It was the same time as our GP's surgery. And there was only one surgery on Mondays. The social worker was calmly reassuring. "It's okay," she told me. "You can take him to the GP the day after. One day won't make any difference."

Brian and I went to the doctor's together, after a nerve-wracking three days. I felt humiliated and ashamed, having to explain why we were there. The social worker had not accused anyone, but I felt that I was the one in the dock — not Brian — because my occasional bouts of anger made me feel guilty, even though Mark and I had formed a close bond, and we had so much fun together. Brian was consistently loving and patient, yet strong and firm, so different from my own father. The doctor too was very kind and gentle. There was no look of suspicion, of

11

condemnation. He looked at Mark's bruises, then he sighed and muttered an impatient, "Is that all!"

Then he asked Mark to climb onto a wooden chair. He did, pressing one shin against the edge of the seat while he hauled himself up. Brian and I looked at each other, our faces mirroring our relief. So that was it! There was a wooden chair in Mark's bedroom that he liked to sit on, to look out of the window. The GP, who knew that I was a fellow-professional, said wryly, "That new playgroup leader must have just done a course on child abuse. Mark is the third child she's sent to me this past month."

We exchanged smiles, and Brian and I left feeling that we had narrowly escaped something very nasty and destructive — but that we were not entirely safe. The doctor wrote, as promised, to the playgroup leader and Social Services, and our names were cleared. But the incident cast a dark shadow over my relationship with Mark. And a new fear was born. Now I was afraid to let Mark, who was accident-prone, play too exuberantly in case he got bruised and I was blamed, and I constantly had to stop myself from inhibiting him.

In spite of the report, we were at last approved as adoptive parents. We were overjoyed, and greatly relieved. Now we could truly think of Mark as our son, and look forward to a future with him. From the beginning, the social workers had said that he could call us Mummy and Daddy, but now we began to feel that we really were his parents.

But then, Mark's natural parents refused to sign the release papers. They were angry because their new baby had just been taken from them, although they had not yet abused him as they had Mark's two older siblings, and they were fighting to get him back. It was not a good time to discuss their letting Mark go. He had now been with us for two years, and we would have to wait another three before we could adopt him without their consent. In the meantime, our social worker went on maternity leave, and we were allocated a new one.

She looked like a witch. She was very tall, with a face that was all points and sharp angles, and long, straight black hair At her first visit, I asked about the new baby as there had been talk of us fostering him as well, and she told me coldly that the baby should never have been taken into care. She believed that all children were better off with their natural parents. And she looked meaningfully at Mark. My blood ran cold. I knew in that instant that it was only a matter of time. Sooner or later she would find a reason to take Mark from us.

The reason was found very quickly. My mother died, after a long battle with cancer. I had only just returned from the funeral when the social worker turned up. She offered me her condolences, then said that she had noticed I was always very uptight when she came to visit, adding that a mother's death is always very stressful, and she didn't think it wise to let Mark stay with me at this time. Besides, Mark's parents now wanted him back, and she had arranged for him to stay with a foster family nearby, so that they could start getting to know him.

She sounded angry and accusing as she bewailed the fact that, as a low income family, dependent on welfare, they hadn't been able to make the long journey to us — ignoring the fact that they had never visited Mark during his first three months in hospital, or during the two years he spent in a local children's home. When I pointed this out, she retaliated by saying that it was very suspicious, our not having taken Mark to the doctor's straight away when there was an allegation of abuse.

Brian and I were distraught. And immediately we appealed, going so far as to ask our local MP to intervene. It was comforting having our church right behind us, making phone calls, writing letters, arranging interviews, even offering to pay legal expenses should we decide to go to court. But we decided not to. Not only would we be fighting a system, and we had no legal claim to Mark, but I felt that I had failed as a mother. The allegation of abuse was totally unfounded, but there had been times when my anger had almost got the better of me, and I had been afraid of what I might do. I had been shocked and horrified at myself, and too ashamed to ask for help. But now I told several friends, and to my amazement they were all very supportive, and all shared similar experiences of almost losing it with their kids.

Following this, our pastor spent three hours with the head of Social Services, producing a batch of testimonials from those very friends and others who had been closely involved with Mark and us; people who had watched him changing and developing into the well-rounded, healthy child he now was.

So great was the protest that the department head agreed to explain the reasons for their decision, and in front of witnesses. But the reasons were so confusing and contradictory that afterwards, no one was any the wiser. It was implied that we were unsatisfactory parents, although they said that we had done nothing wrong, and even agreed that we had worked wonders with Mark. And they said we could apply to adopt again in a year's time, when the dust had settled. But we knew that we wouldn't. And in those days of intense grief following Mark's departure, we felt that there was only one thing that would comfort us: a baby of our own.

Since I had always wanted a large family, I had continued the investigations for infertility, even while we had Mark. I was now attending a specialist hospital in London, and for a long time had been on the waiting list for surgery. I received the letter, asking me to come into hospital, just two weeks after Mark was taken from us. I was to have another laparoscopy followed by a salpingostomy; an operation to remove the fimbria at the ends of the Fallopian tubes and widen the openings.

In a way, I was glad to go into hospital. I wanted to get away from the silent, empty house that was a constant, painful reminder of our loss — although we would be leaving it anyway. Some six months earlier we had put our house up for sale and begun looking for a bigger one, to accommodate our growing family. Our house had now been sold, and we were just waiting for the owners of our future house to move out.

When I came round from the anaesthetic, I knew at once that all they had done was the laparoscopy, not the major surgery I was relying on to get pregnant. And I started to sob, saying over and over, "They haven't done it. They haven't done it."

A nurse tried to comfort me, while another went rushing off to get the doctor. He came at once, and was very kind and understanding. He sat on my bed, holding my hand while he explained that the adhesions were far worse than they had expected, and they hadn't had the right instruments ready. They would do the salpingostomy at a later date.

The delay was more than I could bear, and I wondered what God was playing at. Where was our promised child? I was thirty-four. We had been trying and praying for a baby for over four years. It was more than six years since that day Brian had asked me to marry him and I had begun to dream of having a baby. How much longer would we have to wait? But I kept telling myself that the next operation would solve everything, and we would be comforted for the loss of Mark. Soon now, God would fulfil his promise: he would make me to laugh.

Meanwhile, we were so desperate to get away from our house of sorrow that, when Simon, a bachelor friend, offered us temporary accommodation, we immediately accepted his offer. And we let our house go. The sale was completed the day before my readmission to hospital. And the day after my operation, three couples helped Brian store our furniture in their garages, while he moved in with Simon.

During the operation, the surgeons discovered an ovarian cyst. So, as well as removing the fimbria and widening the oviduct openings, they took away half of one of my precious ovaries. Afterwards, I developed complications. My bladder had become so bruised that it wouldn't function, and at first the bruising and swelling made it impossible for them to catheterise me. I wandered around the ward, trailing my IV stand with one hand and holding onto my distended abdomen with the other, doubled up with pain. And I spent hours in the loo, quietly crying while I struggled to produce a few burning drops.

The nurses soon realised that I was also struggling with some emotional trauma, and when I muttered something about a foster child, they sent the hospital social worker to me. I told her that I couldn't stop thinking about Mark, that I just wanted to know that he was alright, and she promised to find out for me. And then I shut myself in the bathroom and, leaning over a radiator, sobbed until I thought my heart would break.

The hospital social worker got back to me very quickly. She told me that at first Mark had asked for me and Brian all the

15

time. He still talked about me, but was starting to settle down with his new family, which, she explained, was a large one, with several pets. I felt such a stab of envy that I doubled up, and not from physical pain. This was far, far worse. And when she told me honestly that there was no chance of Mark ever going back to his natural parents, I felt that the pain would go on forever.

My physical wound also couldn't heal because, for six weeks, two lengths of plastic tubing had to remain inside the oviducts to keep them open. The surplus few feet, which protruded from the incision wound, had been coiled up and stuck down on my abdomen with masses of sleek — a heavy-duty, very adhesive dressing. As I went through the daily ritual of cleaning the open wound in Simon's none too clean bathroom, I kept wondering how long it would take them to peel away all that sleek and pull out the tubing. And how much it would hurt.

It took a split second! A young and very good-looking doctor removed the lot — sleek and plastic tubing — with one almighty yank and a mischievous grin. The shock propelled me upright in bed, and I instinctively grabbed his hand. Then I just sat there, wondering what on earth had hit me. It must have been a minute later when I realised that I was still holding his hand — and that he was still grinning. I lay back in bed and tentatively smiled back. Thank God, it was over! And now I could start again, trying to conceive. I just wished that we could also move into our new house. But nothing was happening on that front. There was a long chain. And all we could do was wait.

And then, the estate agent phoned to say that the house we were buying had been taken off the market. We were stunned. We didn't know what to do, where to go. We were stranded. But Simon wasn't the slightest bit put out. He told us that we could stay with him as long as we liked. We suspected that he enjoyed having a woman around the house, which was now much cleaner, and being provided with decent meals, and we were glad that the benefit was mutual. Simon was very easy to get on with so, in that respect, we didn't mind staying. But Brian and I wanted to be a couple again — a couple with a baby. We had to find a home of our own.

But that wasn't too easy. It was a seller's market, and we kept getting gazumped. And as the weeks and months passed, and there was no sign of either a baby or a house, we began to think about doing something really different; something that would fill the emptiness in our lives, and help us get over losing Mark. We talked about touring South America for a year, and made some vague plans. But we weren't sure. Perhaps that would be too reckless; too irresponsible. Then we thought about moving to Sweden. Brian, a car designer, had been offered a job there. But that didn't feel right either. And then, Brian was told of the possibility of contract work for the Opel car company in Germany.

Immediately, we knew that Germany was the answer. It seemed right. We felt a peace about it. And we started making enquiries. Brian found work easily, but we had nowhere to live, we didn't know anyone in Germany, and we didn't speak the language. But it was only for a year. If the worst happened, we could find some cheap guesthouse to stay in. And if we couldn't speak the language, so what! We would get by. After what we had been through, that was a minor consideration.

It was now six months since Mark had gone. It was Easter time, the time of resurrection. And we were beginning to feel that we were coming back to life again. It had helped that, thanks to the efforts of our MP, we had received an official apology from Social Services. This had enabled us to start putting the past behind us. And as we prepared for our new life abroad, we believed as never before that soon we would have our promised child. Very soon now, God would make us to laugh.

# Chapter 2

We had planned to move to Germany together, but it didn't work out like that. At the last minute we had bought a house in England after all, primarily to help out our pastor and family who had moved out of the manse and needed temporary accommodation, prior to going abroad as missionaries. Then we had discovered that, to obtain a mortgage, one of us had to be living in the house. So, while Brian started work in Germany, I stayed behind.

Brian moved into a guesthouse frequented by English contractors and known as "The Grot". The rooms were small and the amenities basic, but it was clean — and very cheap. He quickly developed the German style of working: going in early and finishing mid-afternoon. And he spent the remainder of each day traipsing around Frankfurt, from one estate agent to another, looking for somewhere to live. One of the first German phrases he learned was "gar nichts" — "nothing at all".

After six weeks I was able to join him. But we still had nowhere to live. "The Grot" wasn't suitable for couples, and with our money tied up again we could no longer consider spending a year in a hotel. Yet we both felt that God was going before us; that somehow, our going to Germany was tied up with having a baby. And we felt at peace.

And then, the weekend I was booked to fly out with Brian, he turned up at our house in England grinning from ear to ear. A work colleague in Germany had offered us the use of his flat for a week, while he was away. It was a start.

I was very excited as we flew to Frankfurt together, then caught the S-Bahn (local train) for the fifteen km journey to Rüsselsheim. The flat was less than a minute's walk from the station, in Bahnhofstrasse (Station Road), and as Brian lugged one of our suitcases to the flat, I sat on the platform with the rest of the luggage. The station sign — RÜSSELSHEIM — was directly in front of me, and there was a supermarket behind it, with adverts for various food items. Until now, Rüsselsheim had just been a name, a place we had talked about; a dream, not quite real. But as I sat on that platform, looking at the station sign and the German words on the hoardings, I knew that that scene would be imprinted on my mind forever. It was a landmark in our lives.

Apart from a tiny bathroom, the flat consisted of one long room, with a kitchenette at one end, a three-piece suite and coffee table in the middle, and an enormous German bed at the other, underneath the window. I was awakened the next morning by the sound of a road sweeper, and I looked out. To the right, I could see the length of the shopping street. There were outdoor cafes with brightly coloured sunshades over the tables, and I thought, it looks very continental. Then it struck me that it *was* continental. I was in Germany!

That morning, Sunday, we went to a church Brian had discovered. Neither of us understood a word of the service, but we were able to pick out the oft-repeated name of Jesus, and we learned the phrase, "Herr Gott", meaning "Lord God". I liked the sound of it, and I kept saying it over in my mind as we spent the rest of the day exploring. On Monday, with Brian at work, I found myself praying to Herr Gott as I went shopping for groceries, thankful that in a supermarket I had only to take the goods off the shelves, and not ask for what I wanted.

When I returned to the flat, I sat down with my purchases and an English-German dictionary and looked up the German name for each item. Brian had begun learning German by reading the daily tabloid, *Bild Zeitung*. I began by writing shopping lists.

It was May, but the weather was exceptionally hot, and as we trudged around Frankfurt day after day, looking for some-where to live, the heat and dust and noise started to get to me. We looked at several apartments, and twice rushed back to the estate agent to say that we'd take it — only to be told that it had already gone. We were puzzled. We didn't understand the German system; we couldn't work out what was going on. And we began to wonder if coming to Germany had been such a good idea after all.

19

On day five, we looked at an apartment on the outskirts of Frankfurt, in Sigmund Freud Strasse. I smiled at the name, thinking of some of my friends' likely reactions if that became our new address. They had no time for psychiatrists and the like, maintaining that, if you had emotional problems, you just had to trust the Lord and the depression, or whatever, would go away. The apartment was spacious and well maintained, with a balcony overlooking a grove of trees. It was the best we had seen yet, and again we rushed back to the estate agent, a ten minute tram ride away, to say that we'd take it. The woman in charge told us abruptly that it had already gone, and we left feeling more confused and disheartened than ever.

As we stood at the station, waiting for the S-Bahn back to Rüsselsheim, I suddenly experienced a surge of anger and hatred for everything German. And turning to Brian, I snapped, "I'm fed up with Germany! I'm hot, and tired, and my feet are killing me! And I hate the stupid language! And I hate the people! I want to go home."

"Ah!" said Brian, with all the wisdom of his six-week sojourn in a foreign country. "You're going through culture shock. We'll get the S-Bahn later. Let's go out for a Chinese."

I shrugged, and said grumpily, "Alright."

But surprisingly, I felt much better after eating out. And that night, I fell asleep with a renewed feeling that God had everything under control.

The next morning, I had just finished breakfast when Brian returned unexpectedly from work. "Come on," he said. "We're going out. "

"Where to?" I asked.

"To the Immobilien," he said, smiling broadly. "To sign the papers for the flat in Sigmund Freud Strasse."

He had just phoned the Immobilien (estate agent), not being convinced that the apartment *had* already gone. And it hadn't. It seemed that we had turned up just as they were closing, and the only worker left hadn't wanted the bother of going through all the paperwork with a couple who could barely string two words of German together. We duly signed the papers, not

20

really understanding what we were signing, wrote out a cheque for three months' rent, and breathed a sigh of relief. Our search was over. The only problem was that the apartment wouldn't be available for another six weeks. And tomorrow we had to move out of Bahnhofstrasse.

After lunch, Brian went back to work while I went shopping again. By now, I had plucked up enough courage to go into the baker's and butcher's and ask for what I wanted. I was making mistakes, like the time I asked for 200 grams of Leder (leather) instead of Leber (liver), but it gave the Germans a snigger. And they seemed to appreciate my trying. The only absolute disaster was when I bought a packet of Hühnerklein (chicken small) from the supermarket, thinking it meant little pieces of chicken. It turned out to be chicken giblets.

I had just returned with my purchases when Brian came home yet again. He could hardly contain his excitement. "Come on," he said. "We're going to look at another flat."

"What!" I said, rather stupidly.

Then he told me. He had just met an English contractor who had asked him, "Do you know anyone who wants to rent a flat for six weeks?"

He was being transferred to the north for that period, and wanted someone to pay his rent. The flat would be available from tomorrow until the weekend we could move into Sigmund Freud Strasse. This flat was bigger than our current one, having a separate bedroom and kitchen. And it was only one minute's walk from Brian's workplace. It was exactly what we needed.


A few days before moving into Sigmund Freud Strasse, we flew back to England for my father's wedding. Dad was dying with cancer, but he had signed himself out of hospital for the occasion. We went directly from the wedding to Brian's home town, rented a removal van, collected our furniture from our friends' garages, and with Simon to share the driving, set off for Germany, and our new home. We arrived late evening, after a two-day drive, only to discover that when Germans move they literally take everything — even the light bulbs. We spent the evening in darkness, with just one little torch between us.

A week later, I flew back to England again, this time for Dad's funeral. His marriage had invalidated his will, so everything, including all my mother had left, went to his new wife. I was devastated, feeling that my parents had rejected me in death as they had in life. And I started to get depressed. That year, not only had we lost Mark, but I had lost both my parents, my two remaining grandparents, and three other family members. And I still wasn't pregnant. It was all too much.

But somehow I kept going. Two things helped. One was the novelty and interest of being in a foreign country. The other was that we had discovered an American housing area, with a church off base, within walking distance of Sigmund Freud Strasse. We quickly made friends at the church, and within three months found ourselves the leaders of a singles group at the local barracks. Soon, our apartment became an open house to the young soldiers, and I was delighted. I needed someone to mother.

Then, one day, I was shopping in Frankfurt, wearing a raincoat I hadn't worn for some time. I slipped my hand into the pocket, and my fingers closed around a little rubber ball, attached by a length of elastic to a small plastic bat. Mark had won it at a fair, and I had confiscated it because he had kept hitting the ball at my face. Then we had both forgotten about it. Suddenly, tears were streaming down my face, and I stood there, shocked, and confused and embarrassed. Until we lost Mark, I rarely cried, even in private, and here I was, in one of the busiest shopping streets in Europe, openly weeping. People were giving me strange looks and, with bowed head, I dashed into a side street, trying to stem the overflowing of grief.

That weekend, I told our pastor's wife about my experience, and she suggested that I see the counsellor who had recently joined their ministry team. I was dubious about counselling, but I had met Cary and liked him, and he was a Christian. So I agreed. I thought a session or two talking about Mark might help.

Eighteen months later we were still in Germany, and I was still having counselling. It was one of the best things I ever did. Cary helped me deal with my grief, and work through much of the pain and anger arising from my parents' abuse and rejection. He also helped me find new directions in life, and I was now working as a volunteer for the American Community Services, spending two days per week with abused wives, and one afternoon helping with a swimming programme for handicapped children. In some respects, he also helped me come to terms with my infertility. At least, I no longer felt that I wasn't a real woman. But there was still an emptiness inside me that wouldn't go away; an emptiness that only a child could fill.

We had made enquiries about adopting in Germany, and discovered that we had to be resident in the country for at least five years before we could apply — by which time we would be well over the age limit. Our only hope was for me to conceive. So I now began again the painful and humiliating round of tests and operations. I was referred to a hospital in Mainz, and the gynaecologist there wrote to London for my notes. But the London hospital wouldn't send them. So, I had to have another laparoscopy.

On the day of the operation, they prepared me for surgery, gave me a pre-med, and wheeled me down to theatre. Then they left me, alone in a deserted corridor. I was shocked. In my nursing days it had been a strict rule that we never left a patient alone after they'd had the pre-med. I lay there, for what seemed an age, getting increasingly anxious as no one came for me. I could feel my body tensing, and my hands developed a fine tremor. And as time passed and still no one came, my entire body started to shake.

I kept telling myself that it was the effects of the pre-med, but I was beginning to panic. I felt as if I'd been totally abandoned, that I would be left in that deserted corridor for ever, and a scream started to rise up inside me. I was terrified that the scream would escape, and I kept making myself count to ten, telling myself that I could hold on for that long, and then I was allowed to scream. I counted to ten again — and again — and again.

Now my whole body was going into violent spasms, and I was fighting a compulsive urge to get down off that trolley. I felt that I had to get out of that corridor — to find people. I had to know that I wasn't alone in the world. A rational part of me kept saying that I couldn't walk through the centre of Mainz in my op gown, with my bare back exposed, and I reminded myself of the time I'd had the insufflation in England. But another part of me was saying that if I didn't get down off that trolley, I would die.

And then a porter came by. I asked him the time and he told me. I had been there well over an hour. He asked me what was wrong, and I said that I thought they had forgotten me. So he went to make some enquiries. When he returned, he told me that I hadn't been forgotten; it was just that the previous operation was taking longer than expected.

He went, and the panic, that had subsided a little, began building up again. The scream inside me was now a living thing, a monster that I couldn't control. I was half sobbing — strange little moans were escaping my lips — my body was wracked with violent spasms, my legs were jerking, and my hands were tapping a rapid beat on the sides of the trolley — and I couldn't stop them.

Then a doctor came by. He took one look at me, perched himself on the edge of the trolley, and took hold of my hand. I gripped his hand tightly, feeling that I was holding on for my life. He asked me what I was having done, and when I said a laparoscopy, he explained that it was only a minor operation, and he started telling me what was involved. I knew all about laparoscopies. As a student nurse, I had often assisted with them. And this was my third. But I needed him to keep on talking. And I held onto his voice while my eyes held his gaze, and I clung tightly to his hand.

Gradually, the spasms subsided, the shaking became less violent, and the screaming monster inside me began to shrink. Then he said that he had to go. And with a final, encouraging smile and a last squeeze of my hand, he left. I felt utterly bereft. I had never seen this doctor before. I didn't know who he was, and I would probably never see him again. But I felt that I had lost someone very close to me.

It was more than two hours before they finally came for

me. Then I discovered another difference in Germany. They strapped me onto the operating table while I was still conscious. As they fastened me down, I began shaking so violently that I felt as if I was going to jump right out of my body. It was only later that I remembered an occasion when my parents had fastened me down. My mother had pulled my hair to jerk my head back, then pressed a wet flannel over my nose while my father force-fed me with mouldy bread. I had started to choke — I couldn't breathe — and I couldn't tell them I was choking. I'd had a terror of being held down ever since.

Maybe it was the panic of feeling totally abandoned; maybe it was the terror of being strapped down on an operating table. But whatever it was, I had a bad experience with the anaesthetic. As they put me under, I heard a loud noise in my head: a "Waa, Waa" sound that got louder and louder until I thought my head was going to burst open. At the same time, the surgeons started spinning around me, faster and faster until I was sucked into a whirling green tunnel.

The next thing I knew, a nurse was shaking my arm and saying, "Es ist Alles vorbei." ("It's all over.")

I thought, I don't care if it is Alles vorbei. Just go away and leave me alone. I didn't want to wake up. Then I was back on the ward and Brian was holding my hand. We didn't speak. I was too groggy to speak. I just lay there thinking, all this for a baby!

Later, the consultant and two registrars came to see me. For some unknown reason, they asked Brian to wait outside. Then the consultant began talking to me in rapid German. I told him drowsily that I didn't speak German very well, so please could my husband come back in and translate. He agreed, then repeated to Brian what he had just said to me.

As Brian explained that they'd discovered the adhesions to be far worse than they had imagined, the three doctors started to smile, and I wondered vaguely if they understood English and Brian had mistranslated a word. Then I asked Brian to clarify something. Had they done an insufflation under anaesthetic, or were they going to do one? And the three doctors smiled more broadly.

"They did an insufflation under anaesthetic," said Brian.

"That explains it," I replied. "I was wondering why I had a pain in my shoulders."

One registrar now gave a hiccuping little laugh while the other turned away, his shoulders shaking. The consultant had his hand over his face, but I could see that his eyes were dancing.

"I wonder what they're laughing at," I said to Brian.

"I don't know," he muttered, and the three doctors exploded in laughter, while we stared at them, utterly baffled.

"Never will I believe you again when you say that you do not good English speak," said the consultant, wiping his eyes.

We looked at him puzzled, and he said, "Did you not know? You were to each other in German speaking."

Now Brian and I stared at each other. *I* was still groggy from the anaesthetic. *I* had an excuse for not knowing what language I was speaking. But what was *his* excuse? I could only put it down to stress and anxiety. After the first laparoscopy, he always worried when I had to undergo surgery, although he tried not to show it. On that occasion I had experienced an allergic reaction to the muscle relaxant, curare, and had stopped breathing. They had had to resuscitate me. We were paying a high price for our baby.

The doctors now told us — in German — that as air had got through one of the tubes, there was a small chance that I could get pregnant. If I didn't, I could have an operation to remove the adhesions. But they warned me that it would be very major surgery. The operation would take about eight hours. We left the hospital buoyed up with new hope. I was sure I would get pregnant now. But nothing changed. Another month passed; another year. And still, there was no baby.


After three years in Germany, we were asked to help with an international church in Wiesbaden, so we moved to the village of Wehen (pronounced Vayhen), in the Taunus mountains above the town. We had found a lovely apartment, on the top floor of an eight-family chalet-style house, and it had two balconies. The side balcony, set into the overhanging roof, gave us a view over the valley towards the pine-clad hills beyond. But it was

26

the end balcony I especially loved. Our bedroom opened onto one side of it, where it was overhung by a goat willow. And through the patio door of the living room we could look up into the graceful, arching branches of a silver birch. There were more trees behind them, and on the skyline a ridge of pine tops: the edge of a vast forest. We discovered, after moving in, that Wehen means "gentle breeze", or — "labour pains". I became convinced that Wehen was where I would have my baby.

The first thing of significance that happened in Wehen was that the contract firm for which Brian worked closed down, so he was out of work. Most of our savings were tied up in our house in England, so when our tenants moved out and the next-door neighbour asked if he could buy it for his immigrant brother and family, we let it go. We needed the money.

After several months, Brian found a better job, still contracting at Opel, but now as a design checker. And since we had cut our ties with England, we began to think of Wehen as home. But there was no conception, no labour pains, no birth. So, when we had been there two years, and I was thirty-nine, I had my fifth operation for infertility.

In addition to three laparoscopies and a salpingostomy, I had undergone three more operations while in Germany, to straighten my protruding teeth; something English dentists had refused to even consider doing. I was delighted with my new, straight teeth, and the success of the orthodontic treatment and surgery persuaded me to go ahead with the eight-hour long operation to remove the adhesions. It was a last, desperate attempt to get pregnant.

The operation, which actually took twelve hours, went well. But afterwards I discovered, to my horror, that I had to undergo insufflation, not just once, but three times, to ensure that the oviducts remained open. I went hysterical and, at first, no amount of reassurance could persuade me to undergo this ordeal again. But the surgeon was very patient as she explained again and again that it wouldn't be as painful as in England because now the tubes were unblocked. And at last, shaking and sobbing, I allowed myself to be led to the operating theatre. She was right.

It wasn't as bad as in England. But it was bad enough.

We were told that, as a result of this operation, I now had a thirty percent chance of getting pregnant. The odds were against us, but once again we were buoyed up with new hope. At last, after nine long years, God was going to give us our promised child. But nothing changed. Each month was just as it had always been: the fresh hope, the increasing excitement, the worry and foreboding as I experienced the first pre-menstrual cramps, the bitter disappointment and despair, the fight not to give up, and the new belief that next month would be the one.

Another three years went by. And as I passed my forty-second birthday, we started to lose hope completely. And yet, the night God spoke to me, assuring me that one day, like Sarah, I would laugh with joy as I cradled my child, remained clear in my mind. I never doubted the experience. What I now doubted was its reality. I began to think that I had been deluded. And if this experience was a delusion, what about all my other experiences with God — including my conversion? Brian too began to doubt his Christian experience. And from there it was a short step to doubting God's very existence.

By now, we were both studying at the University of Maryland, which ran courses at all major US military bases in Europe. Although non-American, we had been able to obtain study permits, in my case, because of the recommendations of my supervisor at Wiesbaden Army Community Services, where I was now training and practicing as a counsellor. Later, through my contacts, Brian was also given permission to study there. I was majoring in Psychology, and Brian in Business Management. And some of our elective courses, in the fields of religion and mythology, were feeding our doubts.

One term I wrote a paper, trying to prove through teleological and ontological arguments — to myself more than anyone else — that God exists. In my heart, I knew that God can only be proved experimentally, through opening up to his love and grace, and through that love and grace developing and changing into his likeness. But since I felt that my experience of God was suspect, and that I was far from being the loving and gracious person I wanted to be, I decided that I had to rely on academic proof. The facts *were* convincing. But facts were not enough.

In spite of our doubts about God's existence, we continued to be involved with the international church in Wiesbaden. But here, as at university, we could find no answers. Rather, we were becoming increasingly confused. Sometimes, during the prayer time, a picture would flash into my mind; a very clear picture of a pair of arms reaching down to me from heaven. And in those arms was a baby. Either God was reaffirming that I would have a child one day, or he was mocking me. Or, the visions were nothing more than figments of my over-active imagination.

We tried to believe, but as time passed and still I didn't get pregnant, we decided that God *was* mocking us — although we knew that the God of the Bible is not a God who teases his children with false hopes. And then, a visiting speaker, who claimed to be a prophetess, announced that God had revealed to her that he was going to give a childless couple a long-awaited baby. She asked that couple to come forward for prayer.

At first, I reasoned that with 15% of couples unable to have children, there was bound to be at least one such couple in a church the size of ours. So her "revelation" was probably no more than a statistical gamble. But as she waited for a response, I began to feel a surge of renewed hope and excitement. And after a whispered consultation, Brian and I went forward.

"Would you like a boy or a girl?" she asked me, in front of the congregation, and I said that I didn't mind. I just wanted a baby.

But she persisted. "Do you want a boy or a girl? You must be specific when you ask God for something. He will give you whatever you want."

I could feel myself getting angry. Didn't she understand? We had spent almost thirteen years trying and praying for a baby, and when you've been trying and praying that long, the sex of the child is the least of your worries. I wouldn't have cared if it had been bright green with antennae growing out of its head, as long as it was healthy. I just wanted a baby — any baby. She prayed anyway, laying hands on my abdomen, and asked God to give us whatever sex he considered best — why hadn't she done that in the first place? — and we went home feeling heartened and reassured.

Another six months went by. And still there was no sign of our promised child. We were shattered, and we could no longer hold on. It had all been a delusion. There was no God. There would be no baby. There was nothing. We stopped going to church, and no one called to ask why. It was as if we were totally alone in the world; alone with our doubts and confusion, and our grief.

There followed a period of darkness such as we had never known. We felt that we were drowning in a black emptiness, cut off even from each other. But, in that black emptiness, we found God. In the very depths of our souls, we knew that God exists.

When it came to it, we simply couldn't stop believing — and trusting. Even if God had lied to us; even if he had mocked us, dangling the hope of a child in front of us all those years and, as with Tantalus of Greek mythology, whisking it out of the way every time we reached for it, we would still trust him. We would trust him whether we had a baby or not.

# Chapter 3

Now that I had given up almost all hope of ever having a baby, I began putting all my energy into my new counselling career. I soon proved myself able to quickly gain rapport with people of all races and backgrounds, and deal with a wide variety of problems. So I was usually given the more difficult cases: those with deep-rooted problems arising from childhood abuse, and needing more than the statutory twelve sessions. And since I was the only counsellor at Wiesbaden ACS who spoke German, I was also given any mixed-marriage child abuse or custody cases requiring liaison with the German Social Services.

I dreamed eventually of having my own counselling practice, and specialising in counselling adult victims of child abuse. I wanted to give them what I had received from my counsellor: the unconditional love and acceptance of a person's true inner self which, along with professional competence, is so essential if healing is to take place. Then something happened that made me put my career on hold. It was nothing spectacular. It was simply that, for the first time in nine years, I held a baby. But that simple action set off a whole chain of events.

Since that terrible day when Mark was taken from us, I had been unable to pick up a baby — or any child under five. I was so afraid of experiencing again the anguish I'd felt when he'd been dragged from my arms; and when, at the door, he'd turned on me such a lost, bewildered look, and said, "Mummy come too."

I also had trouble coping with pregnant women. Although I always shared their pleasure, I also felt intense envy, and a kind of despair. Just seeing their swelling bodies, the signs of new life within, was a painful reminder of my own emptiness; of my inability to achieve the most basic creative act. So I couldn't bear to be around them for long. As a result, I lost many good friends. I never rejected them outright; I simply let the relationship drift.

And now, my friend, Liz, told me that she was pregnant again, expecting her third child. I experienced the usual mixed emotions, and immediately thought, there goes another friend. But the next moment I decided that, this time, it wouldn't be like that. This time I would face up to and endure my feelings. I was tired of losing friends; tired of being afraid of how I felt or how I might feel. But never would I pick up her baby. That would be asking too much.

I first saw Liz's baby when he was two months old. She was holding him as we stood chatting at a monthly meeting of the Wiesbaden British Women, when her little girl ran up, saying she needed to go to the loo. "Here, hold James for me will you?" said Liz. And before I knew what was happening, he was in my arms.

I braced myself, waiting for the sharp stab of anguish. But it didn't come. What I did feel was a poignant, wistful sadness. And, strangely, a sense of peace and fulfilment. Mark was now in the past. We had loved him and lost him, but now it was completely over. It was time to start again. And starting again meant having a baby of my own.

I was now forty-three, and some of my friends were starting to have grandchildren. So part of me was saying, you're too old. Be content with what you have. And I had a lot: a loving husband, a lovely home, my studies, career, and the freedom to travel. But I could not shake off my longing for a baby. And neither could I forget God's promise.

That evening, I shared my experience with Brian, and we decided to have one more attempt to adopt a baby. I obtained a few addresses of American adoption agencies in Europe, and made some preliminary enquiries. But in every case there was something against us: we were too old, we were the wrong nationality, we lived in the wrong area.... And then, we received a letter from Angela.

I hadn't seen Angela for several years, although we had kept in touch. She and her husband — an Army officer — had returned to the US shortly after I'd had my last operation. Just seeing the letter brought back a flood of memories: her agreeing to, and helping me carry out, some psychological tests on her little girl for a college assignment; her coming to visit me in hospital when I had the adhesions removed, and being so supportive and understanding; and getting a faceful of bushy brown hair whenever she hugged me. Then I opened the letter, and as I read the opening sentence my heart skipped a beat.

Last week, she said, she had been praying for us, and she felt compelled to write to ask if we had ever thought of adopting a baby. If so, she would help us in any way she could. I looked at the date on her letter, and realised that "last week" had been the week I'd held James. For the first time since the prophetess had prayed for us, I felt a stirring of hope.

We immediately accepted Angela's offer and, over the next few weeks, she sent us information from several inter-national adoption agencies. But we never took the enquiries further. Brian and I both had the feeling that we shouldn't rush into anything. God was telling us to wait.

After nearly fourteen years of trying and praying for a baby, we knew a lot about waiting. And we had learned to trust this God whom, only so recently, in our fear and confusion we had decided didn't exist. And when we had come to the place where we could trust him, even if he was mocking and teasing us, it was as if we had stepped through a mirror; the image became the real world, and the world we had always known became a mere image. From this new viewpoint we saw every-thing in reverse — or rather, the right way round. The important became unimportant, and the unimportant took on a new significance; successes became failures, and failures successes; gains became losses, and losses gains.

For me, this experience was especially meaningful. As a new Christian, my fear and insecurity had led me to develop a rigid belief system. I thought I knew God. I had him neatly tied up and labelled. But after nearly thirty years of learning what God is like, discovering what it means to be loved by God and to love him in return, I felt that I didn't know him at all. He was too big to grasp; too big to be put into a little box and labelled. And that was how it should be. And now, this great big wonderful God was telling us to wait. So we waited.

Another three months went by. Then, in February 1988,

we received another letter from Angela. She wrote:

Dear Brian & Jenny;

This is a difficult letter for me to write because I don't know your feelings on this matter. My sister is pregnant and she doesn't want the baby. She is planning to adopt it away. I told her about you, and she has agreed to give the baby to you if you want it. I have included a letter from her to you, she felt that she wanted to write you also.

As her letter says she will be having the baby the middle to the end of July. She has not been to the doctor yet except for the test. She has had 2 other children which have no health problems. Christine has had problems with her other pregnancies but, nothing that you should be concerned about. I KNOW you will need time to pray about this matter. Would you like for me to check with a lawyer about fees, if you would like to call me feel free to do so, and we will help you out in anyway possible. I hope I haven't stuck my nose in where it doesn't belong. If I have just tell me, I'll back off.

Now that I've threw your day into a tizzy, I'm going to change the subject. Thankyou for the lovely Christmas card. It made us want to jump on a plane and come over there right away. I am glad to hear you are getting to do some counseling, finally. [I'd had a break.] I'll be glad when I finally get to do my schooling. Someday far in the future. Well, three kids keep me pretty busy so I had better go for now. Let me know one way or the other when you make a decision. In the meantime, we will be praying for you, that God will lead you in the right decision.

Love & Prayers

Angela, John, and children.

By the time I finished the letter, my hands were shaking with excitement, and I couldn't decide if I wanted to laugh or cry. Then I turned to Christine's letter. She had written on what looked like a page torn from an exercise book, and her hand-writing was big and erratic, the letters going in all directions. It was the writing of a child, although the letter itself showed a certain maturity. She wrote:

Jenny,

Hi. My name is Christine. I'm Angela's sister.

The reason I'm writing is to ask you a very serious question.

Angela has told me about your wanting to adopt a child, because you are unable to have any. Well, to come to the point. I'm going to have a baby around the middle, to last of July, and I am unable to handle children, & personally, I really don't want any.

So, I've decided that, if you would like to pursue the matter of adopting my child, to please write and let Angela know.

If you are allowed to, the medical & hospital expenses would be your responsibility. I don't think there would be a whole lot of lawyer's fees, except to draw up & notarize the adoption papers.

I don't want to get your hopes up, in case there are any complications, but as for myself, there would not be any hassels about it. I wouldn't change my mind or anything. I've been through this before.

Please write soon to let me know. Thank You.

Sincerely,

Christine

As Angela had expected, I *was* in a tizzy. But she was wrong in thinking that we would need time to pray about it. I knew immediately that this was the promised child — as did

Brian when I phoned him at work to tell him the wonderful news. I read the letters again and again. And then I paced the room, too excited to sit still. At last I went out onto the balcony, looked up at the silver birch, and said wonderingly, "I'm going to have a baby!"

Then I looked at the cluster of trees that surrounded the balcony — the willow, a mountain ash, and some Norway spruce — and I said again, still not quite believing it, "I'm going to have a baby!"

A bubble of laughter started to rise up inside me, and as I looked up the hill to the pine forest and gazed at the line of jagged treetops piercing the snow-laden sky, I felt a burst of pure joy. And I shouted out, "I'M GOING TO HAVE A BABY!"

Then I started to laugh. And as I did so, I remembered those words God had given me so long ago: "God has made me to laugh, and all who hear will laugh with me."


We phoned Angela immediately, and she and Christine began making enquiries about private adoption. But no one wanted to know. It was too complicated — a British couple living in Germany wanting to adopt an American baby! So they checked out again the international adoption agencies. Eventually they found one willing to handle our somewhat unusual case, and we began, for the second time in our lives, the long and laborious adoption process. Then, I had two dreams, both in the same night.

In the first dream, I was walking through swampland along a raised, wooden walkway. Although I had no fear of being sucked down into the swamp, I contemplated turning back because I knew that, further along, the walkway came to an end, right at the edge of a ravine with a fast-flowing river, hundreds of feet below. I was afraid of falling into the ravine and getting badly hurt. Then I heard a woman's voice say, "Don't give up. Just keep on going. It will be alright."

I hesitated, wondering if I could trust the woman — and a man whom I sensed hovering in the background — and she said again, "It will be alright. Trust me."

I decided that I would trust her, and I carried on. And

when I reached the end of the wooden walkway, I discovered, in its place, a sturdy metal bridge. I crossed over the ravine safely, although it wasn't until I was some distance away from the edge that I began to feel safe. And then I woke up.

Later that night I dreamed again. In this dream I was climbing a mountain, carrying in my arms a little lamb. So far, I had coped with the steep climb, but I could see that, higher up, the mountainside became almost vertical and there was nothing to hold onto. So, as in my previous dream, I contemplated turning back before I fell and was badly hurt. Then, from the top of the mountain, I heard a woman's voice saying, "Don't give up. Just keep on going. It will be alright."

I hesitated, wondering if I could trust her — and the man I sensed standing behind her. And again, she said, "It will be alright. Trust me."

I decided to risk it, and reached for her outstretched hand — which somehow spanned the vast distance between us — and suddenly I found myself on top of the mountain, with the little lamb still safe in my arms. But I could not feel really secure until I had put some distance between myself and the mountain edge. And then I woke up.

Two days later Angela phoned. She was distraught. She had just heard that a new law had been implemented, forbidding the adoption of babies into or out of their state, and almost over-night all the international adoption agencies had closed down. But, she said, Christine was so convinced that we were the right parents for her baby, she had agreed, if necessary, to come to Germany to have it.

I briefly told Angela about the dreams, and she felt, as I did, that they were a forewarning of this very thing, and an assurance that God had prepared a better way. Now all we had to do was find the woman — and the man in the background — who would enable us to reach our long dreamed-of goal.

Brian and I now began making enquiries about adoption in Germany, and finally he called our local German Jugendamt (Social Services). The man who answered the phone told him that we were way over the age limit but, since we were providing our own baby, he thought there must be something they could do, and he would send us the application papers. He said that he wouldn't be handling it, but the senior social worker in charge of adoptions, who was then on sick-leave: a Frau Klammberg. He was her assistant. When Brian told me, we agreed that this was the woman in the dream — and Herr Schatten the man in the background.

A few days later, we received a daunting batch of forms to fill in; all, of course, in German. And we each had to write an essay, covering every aspect of our lives. Although by this time we both spoke good German, we didn't speak it well enough to answer the many difficult, heart-searching questions prospective adopters tend to get asked, such as, "Why do you want to adopt?"

We had been through all this before with Mark, and we knew that if we sounded too desperate for a baby we would be considered a bad risk. On the other hand, if we sounded too altruistic, adopting to provide a good home for a needy child, we would be considered suspect. It had been bad enough steering a middle course in our own language. But in German! Then, a work colleague of Brian's, a highly literate German who spoke fluent English, offered to translate our English answers into German for us.

It took about two months to complete the paperwork, have medicals, get police clearance, and obtain references. Then, Frau Klammberg arranged an interview at our home.

She suggested a day on which Brian had an exam, but he didn't want to mention it in case she thought he considered getting a university degree more important than adopting a baby. But he did take the precaution of telling his tutor, and was given permission to start and finish the exam late if necessary. We didn't think it would come to that as the interview was scheduled for 3.00 pm and the exam wasn't until 6.30 pm; although he also needed time to eat and then travel the 18 km to the military base, down through the hills and across Wiesbaden, which was always solid with traffic at that time of night.

We had spoken to Frau Klammberg many times on the phone, and she had always sounded very pleasant and friendly.

Now that we met her in person, our view of her was confirmed. But then she began by saying that our age was against us, and my heart sank. It must have been a good ten minutes before it dawned on me that if she had irrevocably decided against us she wouldn't be there. And I reminded myself that, according to the dreams, I had to trust her. She would bring us safely through.

She asked question after question after question, and after a while both of us — as we discovered when we compared notes later — found it increasingly difficult to concentrate in a foreign language. We both wondered at times if we were actually saying what we thought we were saying, especially after Frau Klammberg, who spoke no English, queried the German word "sensible" (pronounced zenzeebl) that Brian had used to describe his brother. After some discussion it became clear, to everyone's amusement, that what we both thought meant "sensitive" actually meant "nervous" or "highly-strung".

This, at least, brought a lighter note to the interview, but towards the end I was starting to feel that it was all too much. I began to experience brain-fade, and as Frau Klammberg addressed some questions to Brian, I switched off completely. When I came to, I realised that she and Brian were discussing the practical details of the adoption. She must have realised that I'd been miles away because she gave me a beaming smile and said, "I have decided to waive your age because of the way you have answered the questions. You have been approved."

The interview had lasted nearly three and a half hours. So, as soon as she'd gone, Brian had to dash off, with no time even to make a sandwich. My brain refused to function for the rest of the evening, and I wondered how on earth Brian was coping with an exam. (He passed with his usual "A".) When he returned we were both too tired to go over the interview. But it didn't matter. We had been approved!

We had now overcome the problem of our age, the legal problems, and the financial problems. Had we adopted through an American agency, it would have cost us up to $15,000 for the agency's fees alone. As it was, we had only the solicitor's fees to pay, Christine's medical expenses, and her air fare to Germany.

The greatest expense was her airfare, which came to $998. But, just before we went to buy the ticket, Brian won third prize in a nationwide business writing competition sponsored by the NCR Corporation. And the prize — $1,000. Now there were just the practical problems to overcome.

In accordance with airline regulations, Christine would have to fly before the thirty-sixth week of pregnancy. Then she would have to remain in Germany for another eight weeks after the birth — the time allowed for her to change her mind — before she could sign the release papers. And we didn't know what to do with her. We couldn't have her staying with us, especially after the birth. That would have been difficult for all of us. And since Christine was very anxious about coming to Germany, we couldn't have her staying in a guesthouse.

But God had that one sorted too. One of my work colleagues at ACS, and someone whom I would have least expected to come to the rescue, told me that she had been thinking about the problem of Christine's accommodation, and she had a solution. Her teenage daughter would be returning to the US for three months during the summer holidays — the exact time when Christine would be in Germany — so Christine could have her room.

The last few weeks of waiting for Christine's arrival were emotionally draining as I battled with two conflicting emotions: a numbing fear and a deep joyful belief in God's faithfulness and goodness. The fear started when I awoke one morning convinced that our baby's life was in danger. For several days I could think of nothing else, and I prayed continuously.

Then Angela phoned. She told me that Christine had been very ill with a virus infection, and had been vomiting contin- uously. They had been afraid that she would lose the baby. But now, they were both fine. I breathed a great sigh of relief. But from that time I could never quite shake off the feeling that there would be something wrong with our baby, although I kept reminding myself that this was our promised child. God wouldn't give us a child who was less than perfect — not when we had been praying for one for over fourteen years.

At last, on a hot June day, we set off for Frankfurt airport to meet Christine's plane. There had been a last minute panic when it was realised that she had forgotten to get a passport. But that had arrived, by express delivery, with two days to spare; and now, in only a few more hours, Christine — or rather our baby — would be here.

We had discovered that Christine was Angela's stepsister, not a blood relation, and we didn't know what she looked like. So when the passengers from the Delta airliner began surging through customs, we looked, not at faces, but at stomachs.

Ten minutes went by, and the surge of passengers became a trickle. Then came one or two stragglers. And finally, a few stewardesses. We asked them if there had been a pregnant woman on board, and they consulted among themselves. One of them thought there had been, sitting at the back. But she wasn't sure. I felt uneasy. Surely someone would have noticed and remembered a woman as advanced in pregnancy as Christine was.

Another five minutes passed — ten — and there was still no sign of her. I could feel my heart beating erratically, and my mouth was so dry I felt as if I was going to choke. But I pushed the fear to one side, telling myself that it *was* Christine the stewardess had seen. Of course it was Christine. But where was she?

# Chapter 4

I don't know how much longer we stood there. Every now and then new information about flight numbers and arrival times clattered into line on the board above our heads. Other planes landed. More passengers surged through customs. More relatives and friends greeted each other.... But for us, time had stood still. We were afraid to move, afraid to speak, afraid to voice our fears. But at last, I managed to drag out the words, "What are we going to do?"

"I don't know," said Brian, with uncharacteristic helplessness. And we stared at each other, like two lost children, as the crowds milled around us.

And then, a little voice at our side asked, "Are you Brian and Jenny?"

My eyes instinctively flew to her stomach. And I was shocked. My professional training told me that she was about thirty weeks pregnant — if that. Certainly not thirty-six. But there was no time to think about that now. I found myself, in the same moment, looking at her face. And we were exchanging smiles.

At first glance, Christine struck me as pretty, but in a very different way to Angela. She had obviously gone to a lot of trouble with her make-up and hair, which was golden blonde and loosely curled onto her shoulders. But underneath the make-up her face had a pinched, sallow look, and her smile revealed teeth that were black and rotting. She was very thin, and I wondered anxiously if she was anorexic. But my predominant feeling was one of overwhelming relief. And as Christine explained, in a pronounced southern drawl, that she'd gotten lost after getting off the plane and had been wandering all over the airport, we welcomed her with a hug and, in accordance with German custom, a bouquet of flowers.

We had arranged that Christine would stay with us for four days before moving in with my work colleague, Isabelle, who lived on an American housing area on the edge of Wiesbaden. We got on well with Christine, but over those four days we became increasingly more grateful to Isabelle for offering to have her, as we discovered just how xenophobic she was. We had been looking forward to showing her some of the local sights, and telling her about German life and customs. But she wasn't interested. Anything new or different frightened her.

Almost as soon as we got back to Wehen, Christine asked about AFN (American Forces Network), and she was horrified to discover that, unlike Isabelle, we couldn't get it up in the mountains. So she spent most of the four days watching American videos. They had to be American. She would not watch English ones — and certainly not German, even when they were purely musical. But we did succeed in getting her out into the local forest for some fresh air, and we took her to the neighbouring village of Idstein, known for its half-timbered, fourteenth-century houses. And, on the third day, we succeeded in persuading her to see the famous Rhine Gorge, only forty minutes drive away. She enjoyed the outing, which we kept short so as not to tire her, but she was obviously out of her element.

We also discovered that Christine would not eat non-American food and, from the first, this became our biggest headache. She would not eat brown bread, of which the Germans have an amazing variety, and Brian spent hours going from one baker's to another, shocking the assistants as again and again he asked if they had any white bread. It was not unheard of, but it was extremely rare. The only vegetables she would eat were black-eyed peas, and they were completely unknown. And, with the exception of bananas, she would not eat fruit. She couldn't tolerate milk products because of ulcers, she couldn't chew meat because of her rotting teeth, and she didn't like fish. She virtually lived on French fries, cigarettes and Pepsi — at least eight cans per day — and my fears for our baby increased.

I was especially concerned because this would be Christine's third baby in three years. Having babies in such quick succession places excessive demands on the pregnant mother, depleting her — and eventually the foetus — of essential nutrients. And when the mother also smokes. . . .

43

Nicotine, I knew, narrows the arteries, including those in the placenta, making it difficult for any nutrients — even when there are sufficient — to reach the foetus. For this reason, smokers usually have small babies. And Christine was no exception. Although she had gone full term with her previous two babies, they had both been small-for-dates: under five pounds. And small babies have less chance of survival.

The nutrient deficit I was most anxious about was calcium, essential for the development of bones and brain tissue, and I immediately bought Christine a big box of soluble calcium tablets. But after the first she refused to take them because she didn't like the taste. I didn't press her, feeling that it was too late anyway. Deep down, I knew that our baby would be born brain damaged; although, on the surface, I rejected the idea, telling myself that God wouldn't give us a damaged baby. This was our promised child — our Isaac. And he would be perfect.

My intuitive fears soon rubbed off on Brian. And we constantly felt helpless and frustrated because there was nothing we could do to ensure that our baby would be born healthy. It was especially galling watching Christine go outside for a cigarette, knowing that every time she lit up, our baby was experiencing foetal distress.

Then we discovered that Christine expected us to pay for her cigarettes. We were horrified, and we told her that she'd have to pay for those herself. But Christine didn't have any money. She had only brought a few dollars with her. So we had to phone Angela to ask her to send some money. We hated having to do this because we knew that Angela was as averse to smoking as we were.

But Angela, as usual, was very understanding. And while she paid for the cigarettes, we stocked up with Pepsi, although this too was very much against our inclination. We did try to get Christine to also drink fruit juice, knowing that so much caffeine is harmful to an unborn child, and that the high sugar content was reducing her appetite for healthy food, but without success.

It was a relief when Christine moved in with Isabelle, especially as they hit it off right from the start. Christine was happy there, and we were so thankful to Isabelle, who over the ensuing weeks became a good friend. Isabelle enlisted the help of another work colleague, and between them they took Christine out and about, to places she felt at home in: the American movies, the bowling alley, the Commissary, McDonalds and other American restaurants, and the American Shopping Center. And she worked very hard at trying to get Christine to eat healthily, and take supplementary vitamins and minerals.

And yet, I was glad of the short time we'd had with Christine. During those four days she really opened up to me, and she shared, in detail, the story of her life. Angela told us later that such openness was unusual; normally Christine kept quiet about her past. She'd had a horrific childhood, and had been abused in every way possible. And she admitted that her second baby, whom she had kept for three months, had been taken from her because she couldn't stop hitting it. Christine was very angry and bitter about this because she had gone to the social worker for help — not to give up her baby for adoption. My heart went out to her. I could understand her anger and bitterness, even though it was now directed at the child she was carrying — our child.

I could also understand Christine's seemingly inconsistent attitude towards her unborn baby. She was doing nothing to ensure that it would be born healthy, yet she had travelled half way across the world, in spite of her fear of anything foreign, because she was convinced that this child would be special. And, she said, she wanted it to have special parents.

Christine had seen a doctor only twice since becoming pregnant, so as soon as possible we took her to my gynaecologist, who was also an obstetrician. Frau Dr Helfer was shocked at how anaemic Christine was, and she prescribed high dosage iron tablets — which Christine didn't take. Then, after giving her a general examination, she called Brian in and showed us the baby on the ultrasound screen. She pointed out the head, back, arms and legs. Then, smiling, she pointed to a tiny protuberance and asked, "Do you know what that is?"

The three of us stared at it blankly, as if we'd never seen such a thing in our lives before, and Frau Dr Helfer's smile broadened. "It's a boy," she said at last.

Christine was amazed. She had been sure it would be a girl. I wasn't sure how I felt. Neither was I sure I'd wanted to know the baby's sex just yet — although it was too late for that now. Then I realised that I truly didn't mind one way or the other. I was pleased that it was a boy — as was Brian. I'd have been equally pleased if it had been a girl. And I smiled inwardly, thinking of the time when I wouldn't have cared if it had been bright green with antennae growing out of its head.

Frau Dr Helfer then told us that Christine was only thirty-two weeks pregnant, not thirty-six, so the baby would not be born for another eight weeks. My heart sank. Apart from some anxiety about Christine needing to stay longer than planned in Germany, and wanting our baby to be born as soon as possible so that we could protect and nurture it, I felt that having to wait an extra four weeks was unbearable.

My friends, when I told them, found this difficult to understand. After all, I'd waited fourteen years for a baby — fifteen, counting from our wedding — so what was another four weeks? But it was like telling a starving man that he'd have to wait an extra four weeks for food. During those infertile years there had been an emptiness inside me, a hunger, that I had tried to minimise or ignore. Now, with a banquet spread before me, the gnawing pain could no longer be ignored. And yet, the picture of plenty, of abundance, filled my every thought and sent ripples of joy from my head right down to my feet. So, in spite of the gnawing pain, I wanted to dance and leap, to shout and sing, as the awed and wondering voice in my brain said over and over, I'm going to have a baby.

Brian was also finding it difficult to wait, although we both found that keeping busy helped. He had his job as a design checker and technical illustrator, and I had my volunteer work. Due to a reorganisation, the counselling programme now came under the auspices of the chapels. My new supervisor, an Army chaplain, was also a family therapist, so I was gaining experience in a very different field. He had provided us with installation passes so we could get on base to attend Sunday services, and get involved in after-church activities. And we both had our studies.

I was now in my final year at university, and Brian in his third year. But while we waited for our son to be born, I suspended my studies so that I could indulge to the full my long unfulfilled nesting instinct. I spent every spare minute in the very shops and store departments I had spent fourteen years avoiding, and I had the time of my life looking at baby clothes and blankets, cots and prams, sterilising units and baby food and all the other requirements for a newborn. When my legs or back had had enough, I would sit in Hertie's restaurant with a cup of coffee before me and a glazed and happy expression on my face, fingering my latest purchase and resisting the urge to announce to the world, "I'm going to have a baby!"

In the evenings I knitted matinee coats and bonnets and bootees, and I frequently looked at the ever-increasing pile of baby clothes, enjoying the sight and smell and feel of the tiny garments. But I didn't need to make or buy very much. We were being showered with gifts and loans of baby clothes and equipment, not only from friends but from people we hardly knew, because, they said, this baby is special.

Brian and I also had a great time browsing through baby books and checking out the meanings of names, as Christine had told us to choose the name from the start, to save the hassle of changing it when the adoption was finalised. But although it was a lot of fun compiling a shortlist of names we liked and considered appropriate, and that would go with our surname, it was also frustrating, because we couldn't agree. Eventually we told Christine that we had chosen either Jonathan David or Stephen James. Her face lit up as she told us that James was her brother's name.

We thought nothing more of this, and two weeks later we told her that we had finally decided on Jonathan David. She became upset and told us that she had written to her brother James, telling him that we were naming the baby after him. And she wanted us to change it. Brian and I were annoyed. It was bad enough finding names that we could agree on, without having to please a third person. Besides, it was our baby! Not hers! But we said that we would reconsider.

In the end, we finished up with three names: Jonathan Wesley James. Jonathan means "Gift of God", and we thought this so appropriate because that was exactly what he was. And since I had first come to know of God's love in a Methodist church, and we both had a great admiration for the Wesley brothers, this name too felt right. And maybe, we thought, our son would turn out to be another John or Charles. Or, like James, the brother of our Lord, a wise and just leader of a local church.

That, of course, was a long way into the future. Our son hadn't yet been born. Although Christine was staying with Isabelle, we saw her frequently, and I always found it difficult to keep my eyes off her bump. It was now growing rapidly, and she was beginning to look near term.

During the waiting period, we took Christine for a pre-arranged interview with Frau Klammberg. First, she saw Christine alone — with an interpreter — then Brian and I joined them. Frau Klammberg told us she was satisfied that Christine knew what she was doing, and had looked at alternatives. Christine had even gone to the trouble of getting the baby's father to sign a release paper; and although this was not legally binding, it was further evidence of her intent.

As Frau Klammberg was speaking, Christine caught my eye, and she drew my attention to her bump. The baby was moving, and together we watched the undulating waves pass over her swollen abdomen. Then we smiled at each other. It was a precious, shared experience that made me feel very close to her — and to the baby. Suddenly, I became aware of Frau Klammberg, the interpreter and Brian looking on and smiling. I had forgotten they were there.

The days crept by, and now, besides the fear that our son might be born brain-damaged, or that Christine would change her mind, or something go wrong with the legal process, was the fear that I might miss the birth of my own baby.

It was now late July, and of course we hadn't been able to have a holiday that year. But Brian's prize from NCR included an all-expenses paid weekend trip to Augsburg, with a conducted tour of the computer works and a presentation ceremony. We had been looking forward to this trip for some time, knowing that it would be the last holiday we'd have together, with just the two of us, for many years. But when at last the weekend arrived, and we were packed up ready to go, Christine phoned.

Christine frequently began phone calls by saying, with her pronounced drawl, "Je-enny, aah haave aa proh-blem."

Every time, I nearly had kittens, thinking that she had changed her mind, or that something major had happened. And every time it was simply that she needed more money or she had some minor physical ailment. Now, as she began, "Je-enny, aah haave aa proh-blem," my heart as usual skipped a beat.

Then she told me that she was having contractions. Now my heart sank. Not now, I thought, just as we're about to go away! I asked her what they were like, and from her description decided that they were merely Braxton Hicks contractions: the painless tightening of the uterus that occurs during pregnancy. And we went ahead with our trip. But I couldn't relax, and I phoned Christine every few hours to make sure that she hadn't gone into labour. I was so afraid of missing the birth of our son. But I also didn't want to miss Brian's presentation. Christine had no more contractions that weekend. But our trip was spoiled; it was not the relaxed and romantic holiday we had planned.

I need not have worried about missing my son's birth. God arranged it so that I was with Christine right from the first real contraction. On the morning of Friday, August 5th 1988, we took Christine for her weekly check-up with Frau Dr Helfer, expecting to then take her straight to the hospital to be induced — although by the new reckoning she still had two weeks to go. But Frau Dr Helfer, who spoke very rapid German with a strong guttural accent, told us that we had misunderstood: this hospital appointment was simply for Christine to look around and meet some of the maternity staff. We were disappointed. But not for long. It was on the way to the hospital that Christine went into labour. And because of the misunderstanding, we had come prepared with our long-packed bag of baby clothes.

The staff at the hospital decided to keep Christine in. But

since she was only in early labour, the three of us were free to stroll around the grounds for most of the afternoon, as her contractions became stronger and more frequent. It was a beautiful sunny day, and there was a sense of leisurely calmness, spoiled only by Christine's periodically wandering off to have a cigarette. Early that evening she was admitted to the labour ward. And while Brian sat in the waiting room reading a Maryland textbook, I stayed with her.

As soon as I walked into the delivery room and saw the old, familiar sights and smelled the old, familiar smells, the professional in me took over, and I automatically began going through the routine checks — mother's colour, respiration rate, the frequency, duration and strength of contractions.... I had to keep reminding myself that this was *my* baby that was being born.

The midwife, Sabine, soon realised from my observations and questions that I was a fellow midwife, and as we chatted, she also discovered my personal interest in Christine's baby. So she kept me fully informed of her findings and reported to me, as one professional to another, the amount of dilatation, the foetal position, the name and dosage of any drugs she administered.... And she asked me if, instead of calling in another midwife to take charge of the newborn, as is usual, I would like to assume that role. Of course, I said yes.

Our son was born at eight twenty-five that evening. All day long I had focused on Christine, coaxing her, encouraging her, wiping her face, holding her hand, as well as acting as an interpreter. But when the midwife cut the cord and placed my son in my arms, I was no longer the midwife. I was a mother.

As I gazed into my son's eyes, tears of joy sprang into mine, and forgetting that I hadn't bathed him yet and he was still covered in blood and vernix, I instinctively bent my head to kiss him. Suddenly, I wanted to laugh, and I remembered that night so long ago when I had heard those words: "God has made me to laugh, and all who hear will laugh with me."

Then I remembered the visions: those pictures of arms reaching down from heaven to hand me a baby. Why hadn't I seen it before? Those were not pictures of natural birth, but of adoption. And what an adoption! How many other adoptive mothers, I thought, are allowed to experience that first gaze, that first kiss? How many are the first to bath and dress their child, the first to feed him? How many other adoptive mothers can bond with their baby right from the very first moments? God was wonderful!

Christine had told me beforehand that she wanted to see the baby but not to hold him. And when I showed Jonathan to her, she exclaimed, "Doesn't he look like Brian!"

And he did. There was no one feature that we could identify with Brian's, but there was a definite resemblance, which later brought Brian in for a lot of teasing. But Jonathan's colouring was more mine: he had dark brown hair, which soon became lighter like his daddy's, and a lovely golden-brown skin. He also had my eyes — as I was often told later — although his are a different colour. Whereas mine are hazel, his have remained a vivid blue. He was a long, thin baby, and had weighed in at a surprising six pounds ten ounces. He was beautiful!

Brian, who had now been joined in the waiting room by Isabelle and the other friend who had helped take care of Christine, was equally delighted with our son. He held him awkwardly but lovingly, and when Isabelle asked if she could have him for a few minutes, I noted with amused pride that, after handing him over, he adopted the classic protective stance: he stood hovering over our son, with his arm stretched out and the palm of his hand flat against the wall, forming an arch around the baby's head. It was a stance I was to see many, many times.

Frau Klammberg had told us that if Jonathan was born at a weekend we could take him home with us, and she would sort out the paperwork on the Monday. So, after the statutory four hours of observation at the hospital, Christine returned with Isabelle, and we set off for home with our brand new baby.

It was now nearly one in the morning and, bursting with pride, I carried my well-wrapped son along the long hospital corridors and across the car park to our waiting car. Brian settled us on the back seat and, as we drove through the deserted streets of Wiesbaden, then up through the silent forests of the Taunus to our village in the hills, it was as if we were all alone in the world — just the three of us, and God. There was a bright moon that night, the sky was full of stars, and God seemed very, very near. I felt so very privileged, so honoured, and so very humble. And I thought, if I died during that drive, I would die happy.

As soon as we arrived home I laid Jonathan on our bed to change his nappy. I had no sooner taken it off when he sent an arch of urine onto our duvet. We giggled, thinking that he was certainly making himself at home. Then, although he had been checked by a paediatrician, I went through the routine tests I had been taught to do as a midwife. And it was then that I realised that something was wrong. I couldn't abduct his right leg. It was too stiff.

Alarm bells began ringing in my brain. But I ignored them, reasoning that it had been a long time since I'd practiced midwifery and I'd forgotten what a baby's muscle tone felt like. Besides, the paediatrician had found nothing wrong with him, so he must be alright. And I reasoned, as before, that we had prayed for this baby a long, long time. After more than fourteen years, God wouldn't give us a child who was less than perfect. Would he?

# Chapter 5

My first three days as a mother were very fulfilling. And blissful, exciting, exhausting, and downright worrying. We discovered that Jonathan had feeding problems: he couldn't coordinate sucking and breathing, and with every mouthful of milk he made a strange choking sound. After only a few minutes he would become exhausted and fall asleep. So I would sit there, waiting for him to wake up so I could give him a little more. Each feed — six a day — was taking up to two hours.

It helped that Brian had taken the week off and was able to take over the routine cooking and cleaning, as well as taking turns at getting up in the night. I had worried that I wouldn't hear Jonathan at night, as Brian had often joked that I could sleep through an earthquake. But, he needed make only the slightest of whimpers and I was instantly awake — while Brian slept on.

Jonathan was also very twitchy. We suspected that he was going through caffeine withdrawal as, on the day he was born, Christine had been really knocking back the cans of Pepsi, and she'd had virtually nothing to eat. We were afraid that his spasms would turn into full-blown fits, so we watched him constantly. Besides all this, in order to cut down on expenses, I was taking charge of Christine's post-natal care, so I was having to make a 30 km round trip twice a day to attend to her.

After the first three days, things became a bit less hectic. I was now going to see Christine only once per day, and to our great relief Jonathan's twitching stopped. But we were becoming increasingly worried about his feeding. He was taking hardly anything, in spite of our patient vigils.

Amazingly, he was a very contented baby, and he didn't seem to be losing weight. And he was so soft and cuddly. I loved to hold him; to feel that warm little body next to mine and smell that lovely baby smell. I didn't mind in the slightest his falling asleep over his feeds. I could have sat with him in my arms for ever, looking at those tiny little fingers, the perfectly formed fingernails, the fragile, downy head, and every exquisite detail of his sweet little face. He was a joy and delight. And, apart from the feeding problem, he was everything I'd ever dreamed of.

By the fourth day, we had become so concerned about his feeding that I took him to a paediatrician in the next village, our local one being on holiday. "You're spending far too long feeding him," she told me, obviously thinking that I was an inexperienced, overanxious mother. "Twenty minutes is perfectly adequate. He'll have taken all he wants by then."

The fact that, in twenty minutes, he'd barely managed 20 ml didn't seem to bother her. I disregarded her advice and carried on as before, thanking God that I was a trained nurse and midwife, and not a novice likely to be influenced by the opinion of an expert.

But now, we were also starting to worry about his eyes. In many respects, he responded to us like any normal baby, fixing his eyes on our faces as we fed him, or following a moving object — although right from birth he'd had a very obvious squint. But at other times he just lay there, seemingly oblivious to everything, gazing vacantly into space. We couldn't make it out. We knew that there was nothing wrong with his hearing. Right from birth he had responded to my voice; and he reacted to different sounds, even with his eyes shut. What we were beginning to fear was that our baby might be blind. But since there were so many times when Jonathan reacted normally to visual stimuli, we succeeded in convincing ourselves that, if there was a visual defect, it was, like the twitching, only temporary; the inevitable result of a diet of hamburgers and chips, Pepsi and cigarettes.

Then, when Jonathan was three weeks old, we took him for a routine test (in Germany) to check his bone development, never expecting for one moment that there would be anything wrong. But there was. The test showed that the bone of Jonathan's right hip hadn't developed properly. The doctor told us that it was a borderline case, and that the only treatment needed was double nappies to force his legs apart and encourage the bone growth on that side. But we were devastated. We didn't know then that, very soon, we would wonder how we could possibly have got so upset about something as trivial as an imperfectly formed bone.

As a result of this finding we now watched Jonathan's movements more closely, and it dawned on us that, when he kicked, his right leg was stiff and jerky. We told ourselves that this was because of his hip problem. But, deep down, I knew that it was much, much more.

It was the day Jonathan was exactly six weeks old that we really began to suspect that there was something terribly wrong with our baby. But that was also the day when it fully dawned on me that Jonathan was not Christine's son; he was mine — mine and Brian's. That was the day we had to go to the American consulate to register his birth as an American national — he was already registered as a German citizen — and obtain his passport.

As Christine had to sign, we had to take her with us, and this would be the first time she'd seen Jonathan since his birth. Brian and I were both apprehensive. We had only another two weeks to go before she signed the release papers, and we wanted nothing to go wrong at this stage. Already there had been some anxiety as Christine had wanted to go back to the States straight after the birth. She had been very homesick and felt that she couldn't face another eight weeks in Germany. She had assured us that she would come back to sign the release papers, but we hadn't wanted to risk letting her go. Although Christine was losing her fear of anything foreign, we weren't sure that she'd be willing to come to Germany a second time.

Isabelle had been wonderful, and had persuaded Christine to go on holiday with her and her daughter, now returned from the US, to stay with some friends of hers in Italy. And she had refused to let us contribute towards the expenses. The three-week trip had broken up the waiting time and helped all of us. And Christine's willingness to stay in Europe, and her entire attitude towards Jonathan, both before and after his birth, confirmed that she would not change her mind. But there was still a niggling little doubt, a feeling of insecurity.

It was while we were waiting for Jonathan's passport to be processed that Christine asked me if she could hold him. From a professional viewpoint, I was pleased. In the long run, I knew, mothers who held their babies before giving them up for adoption, and said goodbye to them properly, were better able to handle any subsequent feelings of guilt or regret. But as a mother, I strongly resented her holding my baby, even for a minute. Nevertheless, I handed him over.

At that moment, Jonathan, who sometimes didn't react to anything at all, turned his little head so that he could fix his eyes on my face. And as Christine and I stood chatting, his eyes never left mine.

After a few minutes, we went to sit down, and he twisted his head around and looked over his shoulder, so that he could still keep his eyes on my face. And when Christine handed him back to me, he gave a little shuddering sigh, snuggled his head into my shoulder, and fell asleep. He had never once looked at her.

I was astounded. Never, in all my experience as a nurse and midwife, had I known a baby to react in this way, not even when picked up by a total stranger. And when we took Jonathan home, with his shiny new passport, my heart was singing.

Maybe I beamed at him more than usual as I changed his nappy that evening. But whatever the reason, for the first time he very noticeably smiled back at me — but only on one side of his face. On his left, his mouth curved into a broad arch, showing his little pink gums, but his right side remained fixed: not a muscle moved. I half returned his smile. Part of me was thrilled; another part was worried sick as a thought, a diagnosis, kept whirling around in my brain.

We decided to inform our local paediatrician, Dr Lieb — now returned from holiday — about this new concern. But over the next two weeks the problem gradually righted itself. So we didn't. I wanted to believe that my diagnosis was wrong, that I *was* being overanxious and letting my imagination run away with me.

We also said nothing to Christine about our concerns.

There was no point upsetting her, especially as we had agreed that it would be wiser if we severed all contact after her return to the States — although of course we would stay in touch with our good friend Angela, who had made all this possible. We had booked Christine's return flight for the day after she was scheduled to sign the release papers.

The day came at last, and while I stayed home with Jonathan, Brian went to fetch Christine from Isabelle's to take her to the solicitor's office. But first he had business in Rüsselsheim, and as Christine was at a loose end, he took her along for the ride. While they were walking down the shopping street, they met Pat, the wife of the work colleague who had loaned us the flat in Bahnhofstrasse, and with whom I had become friendly during the seven weeks we lived in Rüsselsheim. Brian now introduced Christine to her, and without thinking said, "This is the mother of my baby."

Pat's shocked expression and Christine's giggle made him realise what he'd said, and he hastened to explain. But then, Christine had told us that when the new law had been implemented, and the international adoption agencies closed down, she had considered saying that Brian was the father, thinking it was the only way she could give her baby to us. Angela had told her that we would never agree to that, and we had told her the same. Nevertheless, we had been touched by her firm belief that we were meant to adopt Jonathan, that we were the right parents for him, and by her unshaken resolve to make the adoption a reality.

After chatting to Pat awhile, they carried on down the shopping street. It was market day in Rüsselsheim, and as they passed a clothes stall, Christine stopped to look at a calf-length, grey winter coat. She had obviously fallen in love with it, so Brian promptly bought it for her as a thank-you gift. The stall keeper pointed out that there was a flaw in it, but Christine didn't mind. She said that she could easily repair it. And she was delighted with her gift. An hour later, in the presence of Frau Klammberg, she signed away her baby. As she had promised all along, there was no hassle.

Later, as Brian and I told each other about our day, it struck us as bizarre: a baby in exchange for a coat! And a flawed one at that. We were still thinking about it the next day as we picked Christine up from Isabelle's and, on the way to the airport, called in at the American Child Development Center where we had left Jonathan. Two weeks previously I had resumed counselling, after six weeks maternity leave, and I had obtained special permission to use the CDC for the two days I worked. And it was there that Christine held her baby for the last time. I watched her face closely and was surprised to see so little emotion on it. She didn't seem at all upset.

I was concerned about her, wondering if she was making a brave effort to hide her feelings. And at the airport, as we waited for her boarding call, I commented that she must have very mixed feelings about leaving her baby behind.

"No-o," she drawled. "He wa-as a bur-den the whole taame ah was carrying him. Ah couldn't wait for him to be born — so ah could be rid of him."

I felt a welter of emotions — anger, sadness, relief, gratitude. Christine had told me, during her first four days in Germany, that she had considered having an abortion, and I was so thankful that, in spite of Jonathan being an unwanted burden, she had carried him to the end. But how could anyone, I thought, think of Jonathan as a burden? He was a delightful baby, so contented and so responsive, always gurgling and chuckling. He was a joy and delight; a wonderful dream come true.

It was a relief to see Christine go. She and I had become close during the four months she had been in Germany. It was inevitable that we should as we had shared so much, and I had been so many things to her: friend, counsellor, midwife, and mother of her child. But Brian and I wanted our baby all to ourselves. While Christine was still in Germany we felt that, in a way, she was an intruder. But now, at last, there was just the three of us. We were a normal family: a couple with a baby.

We were even more relieved when, a few days later, we received a copy of the official release form. And we were thrilled to discover that, rather than merely stating that Christine had released her baby for adoption, as is the norm, it was specified that she had released him to be adopted by us, Brian and Jennifer Minney. We still had a long time to wait before the adoption was finalised. And, as in my two dreams, I couldn't feel entirely safe until it was. But now we were beginning to feel that legally, as well as emotionally, Jonathan was well and truly ours.

That same day, we took Jonathan to England, to show him off to the relatives. We were so excited! Nothing could dampen our spirits, not even the stormy channel crossing. Severe gale force winds rocked the ship as it plunged and leapt through the inky waves. We sat in the cafeteria, holding on to our plates and bags to stop them sliding up and down the table, while Jonathan gurgled and cooed in his baby rocker, which we had placed in a safe place, enjoying the continuous movement. Every few minutes crockery leapt over the raised edges of the tables and crashed onto the floor, to rounds of applause from the passengers; while those brave souls who tried walking around, staggered about drunkenly, colliding with each other, lurching into tables and walls, and grabbing anything within reach to stop themselves being hurled onto the heaving deck.

We would have stayed put for the entire trip if Jonathan hadn't needed his nappy changing. I lurched off in the direction of the Ladies, then edged my way down the long passageway, using the walls for support while holding on tightly to my precious bundle. When at last I reached the Ladies, I found that there was nowhere to lay Jonathan down: just a narrow ledge meant, I think, for bags. Certainly not for babies. Not knowing — as I found on subsequent crossings — that there were special baby changing areas, I placed Jonathan on the ledge and, holding on to him with one hand, I cleaned him up with the other. Sheer will power kept me on my feet because I knew that, if I fell, Jonathan would fall too.

We arrived in one piece after a gut-wrenching journey that took an hour and a half longer than usual. Then we spent another hour being tossed around outside the harbour wall, as it was considered too risky to try manoeuvring through the entrance. But at last the winds dropped a little, the ferry docked, we collected our car, and set off on the last leg of the journey to Brian's parents.

They fell in love with their new grandson at once, as Brian's brother and family did with their new nephew and cousin. But then he was the kind of baby it was easy to fall in love with. He had a permanent smile on his face, and it took very little to set him off gurgling and cooing and chuckling his infectious little chuckle. My friend Pam, whom I had first met at the time I met Brian, also took to him immediately. She had followed avidly the unfolding Jonathan story, and now she summed up everyone's feelings when she said, "It's as if Jonathan has always been there. He belongs."

Later, we went up North for a few days, and my sister and two great aunts were equally delighted with Jonathan. But, knowing my family, it was inevitable that there would be those who showed not the slightest interest in our son, and made excuses not to see him. I was hurt and angry. One day, I knew, we would tell Jonathan the amazing story of how he came to us, and we hoped our love would cushion him against the rejection he must feel when he learned that his natural mother hadn't wanted him. But his being rejected by members of my family as well, just as I had been rejected, didn't bear thinking about.

While we were in England, Jonathan developed mild diarrhoea, which I put down to the change of water. But when the problem persisted after our return to Germany, I took him along to the paediatrician. Dr Lieb examined him. Then, suddenly, he waved his hand in front of Jonathan's eyes. There was no response. He tried again. And again. But still Jonathan lay there, totally unresponsive, his eyes fixed on the ceiling. "Have you noticed if his eyes ever follow moving objects?" the doctor asked me, and I explained how, sometimes he responded, and at other times he didn't.

"You must take him to an eye specialist," he told me. "As soon as possible. If you like, I will make the appointment for you."

"What's wrong?" I asked, as an icy chill gripped my heart.

60

The doctor turned away, sat down at his desk, and concentrated on writing up his notes. "I don't know," he said at last, keeping his face averted.

He was obviously upset, and this, more than anything, brought it home to me that there really was something radically wrong with our baby. And the thought hammering in my brain was the one that had tormented me at the start: that Jonathan might be blind.

As soon as I got home, I phoned Brian at work, and he came home immediately. Then, as Jonathan slept, we held each other, vowing that never again would one of us take Jonathan to the doctor without the other, not even for a routine check. In future we would go together, and we would face together whatever there was to face.

Our appointment with the eye specialist was for the very next morning. I was relieved it was so quick. I don't think I could have tolerated a longer wait. But that evening seemed to go on for ever. We were terribly afraid.

As the specialist examined Jonathan's eyes, we sat there, helplessly watching her, bracing ourselves to hear the worst. "He's a bit long-sighted," she said at last. "And of course he has a squint. But otherwise, his eyes are fine."

The relief we had felt when Christine signed the release papers was nothing compared to this. We were giddy with it. And we staggered out of her practice into the bright autumn sunshine, fighting back tears of joy.

But our joy was short-lived. Two days later she phoned us. "I have been thinking," she said. "There is nothing wrong with his eyes, but he might have some brain damage. I suggest that you take him for a brain scan."

Again, there was the waiting, the agony of suspense, the dread of what they would find. I could now no longer ignore the phrase, the diagnosis, that had haunted me ever since that day when Jonathan smiled at me for the first time: cerebral palsy. But I told myself that it couldn't be. God wouldn't be so cruel. If we'd wanted a handicapped child we could have adopted one years ago. God wouldn't have kept us waiting all these years — for this!

At the clinic they sedated Jonathan, then placed him under the scanner, which photographically sliced through his brain, as if through a loaf of bread, taking pictures of each slice. Then, a white-coated doctor handed us a large, sealed brown envelope, and told us to take the pictures to a neurologist. "He will interpret them for you," he said.

We stared at him, wanting to ask him what the pictures showed, yet afraid to ask. He obviously sensed our fears, but didn't seem inclined to relieve them. He gave us both a firm handshake then moved briskly away. But just before he went, he gently touched Jonathan's head, and a look of profound pity flitted across his face. That look and action confirmed for me, as Dr Lieb's reactions had, that my fears for Jonathan had not been the product of an over-active imagination, but a deep instinct; an inner knowledge of a terrible reality.

The next day we phoned a neurologist and, having made an appointment, handed in the sealed brown envelope. We were longing and dreading to know what was inside, but we had to wait yet another two days.

When at last we got to see the neurologist, a man who looked to be in his late sixties, he ushered us into his office, shook our hands, and then indicated the pictures of Jonathan's brain, displayed on an illuminated screen.

"Well, as you can see, your son is severely brain damaged," he said brutally. "This is the worst picture." And he pointed to one that showed nothing at all. Nothing but a black emptiness where there should have been healthy brain tissue.

I promptly went into a state of shock. I didn't hear what else he said, or see the other pictures. (Brian told me later that well over half of them were normal.) My eyes were fixed on the black void — the nothing. And as I stared, the picture embedded itself in my own brain, so that for weeks to come that black emptiness tormented even my dreams.

Gradually, as if through a fog, I became aware of snatches of conversation: "Right-sided hemiplegia — disturbed vision —

spasticity — difficulty swallowing —"

I tried to clear my head, to focus on the facts. And suddenly, the fog lifted, and very clearly I heard Brian ask what had caused the brain damage.

"It could be one of several things," the neurologist said casually. "Or a combination. The damage occurred during pregnancy — probably during the last three months."

Then, turning to me, he asked if I had taken any drugs while I was pregnant. I stared at him stupidly, and Brian explained that we were adopting Jonathan, and that the natural mother *had* experimented with LSD and smoked pot. But, he said, as far as we knew, this was before she became pregnant. Then Brian told him about Christine's smoking and totally inadequate diet. The neurologist shrugged and said, "That's probably it, then."

He now examined Jonathan, while muttering something to the effect that there may also have been some trauma that had stopped the brain from developing. *My* brain went blank. I could think of nothing. It was months later when I thought of the virus infection, and wondered if that had been just one thing too many.

Then Brian asked him the question that, for the past few minutes, had been whirling around in my brain: "How will this affect Jonathan?"

"Well, he will probably never walk — or use any of his right side," he replied offhandedly. "He might also be mentally retarded. And he'll probably be epileptic. If I were you, I would put him in a home and forget him."

# Chapter 6

I stood there, staring at the neurologist. I thought I must have misunderstood him — he was, of course, speaking German. Put our precious, long-awaited son in an institution! Suddenly, the full impact of his words hit me, and I was so angry I wanted to hit him; that smug, pompous, unfeeling brute who talked about our son as if he were a faulty piece of furniture we could return to the manufacturers. To keep my feelings under control, I deliberately turned my back on him, and concentrated on dressing Jonathan.

Brian and I didn't say a word as we left the surgery, headed back to the car, and began the return journey home. It was a beautiful drive, up a winding mountain road through forests of beech and pine. But today I noticed nothing; nothing except Brian's white knuckles as he gripped the steering wheel. He was obviously as furious as I was. And I *was* furious. Anger was now rolling over me in great engulfing waves. Anger at the neurologist, anger at Christine, and anger at God. We had prayed for over fourteen years for a baby, and instead of the perfect, healthy child we'd expected, we had a severely brain-damaged one who would likely spend the rest of his life in a wheel-chair; drugged to the eyeballs to keep his fits under control.

Suddenly, abruptly, my blazing fury turned to a cold determination. And, matter-of-factly, I faced a future that, as far as I could see, held nothing but hard, unmitigated work. Well, Jenny, that's the end of all your dreams, I told myself. But you've no time to mourn; you've a job to do. I was determined to prove that neurologist wrong. Jonathan would walk. We'd make sure of that — and more. We would ensure that one day he'd be able to live his own life — without us — totally independent. As for his being mentally retarded, anyone could see that he was a bright, intelligent baby. And one day, I vowed, if it was what Jonathan wanted, he would go to university. I tried not to think about his being epileptic.

I didn't need to ask Brian how he felt. But I asked him anyway. He gripped the steering wheel harder and, with what for him was strong language, said exactly what he thought of the neurologist. "That was our son he was talking about," he fumed. "You don't get rid of your own child just because there's something wrong with it."

He took a shuddering breath, then said more calmly, "And as for saying he's mentally retarded, any idiot can see that he's bright and alert, even if he doesn't always follow things with his eyes. And he'll walk. One day, he'll walk — and run and jump and do all the things other kids do."

I agreed, wondering at the back of my mind if we were being unrealistic, if we were denying the reality because it was too terrible to accept. And yet, with all the shock and grief and anger, I felt a sense of peace. God was with us. He knew what he was doing. We could trust him. The anger I'd felt towards God had disappeared as quickly as it came. God hadn't made Jonathan the way he was. Human sin had done that, directly or indirectly. Certainly, God could have over-ruled. He could have healed Jonathan in the womb and made our baby as perfect as he was intended to be. But he had chosen not to. I didn't ask why. It was the wrong question.

The anger I felt towards Christine took longer to dissipate. With her it was more complex because I was also angry with those who had abused her. I was angry with all abusers, especially with all mothers who hurt or rejected their children. It should never have been like that! It was all wrong! And yet, I could understand why mothers abused. I remembered how I had sometimes been with Mark, and I thought of the hate I had often felt towards myself. Had I become pregnant in my early twenties, like Christine, and had I never come to know God's love and acceptance, I too might have been guilty of foetal abuse. Yes, I was angry with Christine, but I could not condemn. And because I felt such compassion for her, knowing how much she had suffered in her short life, I could forgive.

The anger I felt towards the neurologist remained for a long time. And it was this that kept me going. It was the driving force, the determination that enabled me to cope with the endless round of physiotherapy, with the constant setbacks, and with the feelings of grief and sadness that never entirely went away.

But now, as we wound our way up Eiserne Hand (Iron Hand) to our village in the hills, I also felt a sense of privilege. God had chosen us to care for a very special child — a twice-special child. He was special because he was adopted, and he was special because he had exceptional needs.

The more I thought of how God had picked us out to be Jonathan's parents, the more honoured I felt, especially in view of my background. I knew, because of my studies, that people who have been abused have a tendency, for various psychological reasons, to abuse their own children — although it certainly doesn't follow that they will — in spite of its usually being the last thing in the world they want to do. The risk is increased when the child is in any way different, such as being deformed or handicapped. And when there is also stress and isolation to contend with, the combination is potentially lethal. Adopting a child, I had discovered, is not the easy way to have children. I was feeling as if I'd had a fourteen-year very difficult and painful pregnancy, followed by several weeks of labour as I fluctuated between periods of relaxed calm and tense anxiety. And my two closest friends, who had been so supportive while we were going through the adoption process, had recently moved abroad. God knew all this. And yet he trusted me. And when I thought about it, I realised that I also trusted myself. The fear that had often tormented me when we'd had Mark had gone. And gone, I hoped, never to return.

The first thing we did when we arrived home, after settling Jonathan down to sleep, was phone our chaplain. We knew that we were going to need all the support we could get. The chaplain dropped everything and drove out to our village immediately, and we were so grateful for his concern, his wisdom, and his loving support. He shared our feelings of anger at the neurologist's heartless suggestion, but when I told him that I had been having doubts, not about keeping Jonathan, but about whether, at my age — forty-four — I would be able to cope with a severely handicapped child, he simply said, "Don't limit yourself, Jenny."

I knew he was right. I would cope. We both would. However stormy the way ahead, we would stay on our feet — for Jonathan's sake.

Our friends at the church were equally supportive. The chaplain spread the word around, and many phoned us, offering their prayers and practical help. And at church the following Sunday we were overwhelmed with all the love and concern that was showered upon us. Some people obviously didn't know what to say. But when they put their arms around us and cried with us, that said it all.

And now began, along with all the joy and laughter, a long period of mourning: grief for the dream child who never was, and sorrow for what our real-life child would have to face as he grew up. Parents who have given birth to sick or deformed babies usually go through three distinct phases, as for any type of bereavement. First there is a feeling of unreality and disbelief; then, a period of anger; then, as the reality of what it means to care for a handicapped child, day in and day out, begins to dawn, there is a period of depression, often accompanied and exacerbated by feelings of guilt. Finally, with faith, support from people who care, and the healing balm of time, there is acceptance.

Of course, people vary in how intensely and for how long they experience the three phases, which aren't always sequential. In our case, probably because, at some level, we had realised from the beginning that something was wrong with our son, the period of disbelief lasted only a matter of minutes. Almost our first feeling was anger, and anger kept us going for a long time. Depression didn't hit until much later, and then it was short-lived; in my case, probably because, unlike natural mothers who give birth to handicapped children, I could not torture myself with thoughts of what I might have done wrong during pregnancy. Although, strangely, Brian and I did go through a period of wondering if, in fact, the damage had occurred after birth, and we thought of the most far-fetched reasons for Jonathan's disability.

But what helped most of all was the love and care of

others. When we wrote to tell friends and relatives that Jonathan had cerebral palsy, we received many beautiful cards and letters, which we got out and read over and over whenever we hit a low point. And always there were people at the end of the phone — people who would listen as we poured out our pain and confusion, people who offered to baby-sit so that Brian and I could have time to ourselves, and people who helped with Jonathan's physiotherapy. We were experiencing as never before what true Christianity is all about: it is all about love.

As well as surrounding ourselves with positive, caring people, we also found out everything we could about Jonathan's condition. Since we were both still studying at the University of Maryland, we had access to the American library, and we read up all we could about the various types of cerebral palsy, and we bombarded our paediatrician, neurologist — we found a different one — and physiotherapist with questions.

Another thing we did, of course, was inform Frau Klammberg. She was sympathetic and encouraging — her own daughter had had to have physiotherapy because of coordination problems — but I don't think she realised just how badly damaged Jonathan was. We had been given Jonathan's diagnosis just three days before we were due to sign the adoption papers, which, Frau Klammberg had explained, legally committed us to adopting him. But now she told us that if we found that we couldn't cope, she could, in spite of our having signed, explain to the judge that circumstances had changed and recommend that the adoption not be approved. But we were sure that this necessity would not arise. There was no question of not coping. Jonathan was our son: our long-promised son. We would have to cope.

Until the adoption was finalised, the Jugendamt , as represented by Frau Klammberg, was Jonathan's legal guardian. We were merely acting as foster parents. But right from the beginning, Frau Klammberg had given us a completely free hand with Jonathan, and she came to see him only at our invitation. There was none of that constant checking up on us that we'd had to endure as foster parents in England. And now she left

Jonathan's medical care entirely up to us: we could decide which doctors to take him to and when, and what treatment he should undergo. God had told me, through my dreams, that we could trust Frau Klammberg, What God hadn't told me was that she would have implicit faith in us. This mutual trust made for a good relationship that helped smooth many of the rough times ahead.

We went to a solicitor in Wiesbaden to sign the adoption papers, and discovered, to our relief, that he spoke English. As he went through the forms with us, he explained the legal jargon; bad enough in our own language, but in German totally incomprehensible. Basically, adopting Jonathan would give him all the legal rights of a legitimate, natural child. And, of course, it would give us all the rights and responsibilities of natural parents. When he had gone through everything, the solicitor handed Brian a pen and asked us if we were willing to sign. We said yes. That was what we had come for; what we had waited fourteen years for.

First Brian signed. Then he handed the pen to me. But just before I signed, I hesitated. It was not because I had any doubts about the step I was about to take. It was because this would be a far greater commitment than anything I had ever envisaged. I might be signing away all my rights to a normal life: I might have to give up my work and my study and dedicate every moment, until my dying day, to caring for my handicapped son. I steeled myself, and as I stared resolutely into an uncertain future, I signed. Then, I gave a sigh of relief. We had done the right thing. There was no doubt about that. But as we left the solicitor's office, with the weight of our grief still heavy upon us, we were both in tears. It should not have been like that.

God had promised me, as he had Sarah so long ago, that he would make me to laugh, and that all who heard would laugh with me. It seemed instead that God had made us to cry, and that all who heard would cry with us. And yet, even then, in those grief-filled days following Jonathan's diagnosis, our greatest comfort was Jonathan himself. Right from the beginning he had been a contented baby, and from that first lop-sided smile had

69

developed a permanent grin. Happiness simply radiated from him, to such an extent that it was impossible to be near him and not feel blessed. We hoped he would stay that way.

Before Jonathan was born, I had written in my baby book, under the heading ,"Our hopes for baby's future":

We hope that our baby will come to know and love Jesus as we do. We also hope that he will be healthy and happy and that he will grow up feeling secure and confident, and that he will always be curious about this interesting and wonderful world he is coming into.

Now, after returning from the solicitor's, I re-read this entry, and it took on a new, deeper meaning. We were now more concerned than ever with every area of Jonathan's life — spiritual, emotional, mental and physical. And because of his irreversible brain damage, we would work harder than ever to assist his development in each of these four areas.

Our immediate concern was to get Jonathan started with physiotherapy as soon as possible, to help him gain some use of his paralysed right side. We didn't know what we were aiming for; we didn't know what was a realistic goal. But one thing we were certain of: we would get him walking, no matter what it took or how long it took. We would prove that neurologist wrong.

Dr Lieb recommended a physiotherapist in our village, but she was in the process of moving her practice. And then it would be Christmas. I didn't want to lose even a day, so, using my limited nursing knowledge, I began gently putting Jonathan's stiff limbs through a range of movements. And Brian and I spent hours stroking his affected right side, using a variety of instruments: our hands, soft fluffy toys, hard plastic toys.... We had been told that there would be some sensory deprivation, and not knowing how much, if anything, Jonathan felt when we stroked his right side, we also stroked his good side. We could then be certain of his getting some enjoyment from the exercise.

I was so glad now that I had spent so many hours simply holding Jonathan, stroking and caressing him. My one disappointment with having an adopted baby was that I hadn't been able to breast-feed him, although I had heard that, after six weeks or so, adoptive mothers who put their babies to the breast can produce a little milk. I had given it a try, but Jonathan's feeding problem had made this impracticable. So after two weeks I had given up. But at least, during that time, he had experienced the closeness and nurture of a mother's breast. And perhaps this too, I thought, would have contributed to enhancing his sense of touch.

Meanwhile, I was getting ready for Christmas. Traditional British Christmas fare, such as mince pies and Christmas cake and puddings, are unknown in Germany, and some ingredients, such as suet, unobtainable. So a group of us British expatriates had begun our own tradition of a mincemeat making afternoon, with whoever had made the most recent trip to England supplying the missing ingredients. This year I took Jonathan along, and placed him out of the way in his little rocking seat. But he didn't stay there long. As he sat there, gurgling and cooing and beaming at everyone, there was a scramble to pick him up and cuddle him. Everyone wanted to hold him. And from then on, at our annual mincemeat making, holding or playing with the baby became the favourite assignment, far preferable to chopping the dates or grating the apples.

A few days later, I made my cake and puddings, and as the house filled with the rich aroma of baking, I wondered about Jonathan's sense of smell. Had that too been affected? There was no way of telling. I wondered again as we brought home the Christmas tree, and the house filled with the heady scent of pine, bringing the comforting forests that encircled our village right into the living room. But, whether he could smell it or not, Jonathan was all eyes as we draped the branches with tinsel and hung traditional German wooden ornaments, and he gazed in wonder at the silver star on the top. And when we switched on the fairy lights, he kicked his little legs and waved his one good arm, laughing and squealing with delight.

Brian's parents spent Christmas with us. We had told them about Jonathan's condition, and naturally they now wanted to know all the ins and outs of it. But we didn't want to talk about it. Not then. This was our first Christmas with a new baby, and we wanted to make the most of it. We didn't want to discuss, as they did, paralysed limbs and wheelchairs, learning difficulties and special schools, and epileptic fits. But, whether we talked about it or not, I couldn't entirely shake off the picture of Jonathan's missing brain. I would look at the Christmas tree and see a picture of nothing. I would look through the patio door at the silver birch arching over the balcony, and see a black void. Even when we went out for walks, instead of the green, fairy-tale wonder of the beech forests or the dark, brooding mystery of the pine forests, I would see that terrible picture of nothing. It was there while I served mince pies, it was there while I cooked the turkey, it was there while we opened our presents. ... There was no escape.

And yet, it was a wonderful Christmas. Since losing Mark, Christmas had always been a sad, empty time for Brian and me, and we had tried everything, even going to North Africa for the Christmas period, to try to avoid it. But there had been no avoiding it. Even there, Father Christmas had turned up on a camel, and we'd had to walk away because we couldn't bear to see the children scrambling for their presents.

But now I was a mother. And as a mother I had the fun of sorting out my son's presents on Christmas Eve, and putting them into a pillowcase; and seeing the excitement, hearing the squeals of delight as we opened them for him the next morning. And for the first time in ten years, I could be a child again, lying on the rug going "brrmm, brrmm" with Jonathan's squeaky car, giggling with him as I rolled his see-through rattly ball, and reading to him for the first time, from a baby's board book, the story of that very first Christmas: of the baby in the manger, with the moo cows and baa lambs — and some clucking hens and squawking ducks thrown in for good measure. I was in my element.

Christmas 1988 was over too soon. And now it was New Year's Eve. In Germany, most people go out into the streets or

72

onto their balconies at midnight, and light fireworks. Brian and I had developed the habit of getting everything ready at about 11.40 pm: mince pies warming in the oven, drinks ready to pour, and extra woollies, along with coats, hats, scarves, gloves and boots, ready to scramble into when we'd welcomed in the New Year with a toast and a hug and kiss. Then, at a few minutes past midnight, we would dash outside onto the side balcony, from where we could look out across the valley and see the villages of Hahn and Bleidenstadt, nestling among the hills on the other side. It was a superb vantage point for watching the fireworks.

And now, as the sky filled with explosions of silver stars and trails of blue and red flame, I made up my mind that one day, Jonathan would stand on this balcony with us and watch the fireworks bringing in the New Year. I wondered which year that would be; how long it would be before he would be able to stand up. I also wondered, with a shiver that wasn't altogether due to its being below freezing, just what, if anything, he would be able to do before the next New Year.

# Chapter 7

It was the first week in January when I took Jonathan for his first hour-long session with the physiotherapist. Frau Trepp-Jung had moved her practice to the other end of Wehen, a sprawling village built along a T-shaped valley, and nestling among the densely forested hills of the Taunus. It was a good half hour's walk to her practice, and from that first session I pushed Jonathan's pram, in all weathers, down into the valley and up the hill on the other side for his twice weekly appointment with her. But the bulk of the work was done at home.

We discovered that Frau Trepp-Jung used the Bobath method of physiotherapy, the aim of which is to encourage the brain to produce new neural pathways to compensate for the missing ones. And to do this it is necessary to repeat the same movements over and over, day in and day out, month in and month out, and sometimes year in and year out. We had now realised that Jonathan could move his head in only one direction: to the right. So our first task was to teach him to turn his head the other way and to roll over:

Turn his head to the left, move his right arm across his body, bend his right leg, slowly move his bent leg over the other leg, push the rest of his body over, pause, slowly roll him back again, straighten his right leg, put his right arm by his side, straighten his head. Turn his head to the left.... I used to roll him over in my sleep.

The endless physiotherapy meant that I had little time for myself. But since I was so near to graduating, and I felt that it was important to have *some* mental diversion, I had decided not to give up my studies. But the only way I could cope with university and Jonathan was to prop a textbook up on his cot, and study while I went through his exercises; that is, until I hit on the idea of making study tapes. I had recommenced with an elective philosophy course, "Ideas Shaping the 21st Century". And the main ideas of freedom, equality and individualism soon became embedded in my brain, along with the sequence of movements I was trying to imprint in Jonathan's:

The philosophy of individualism — turn his head to the left — the legacy of Protestant theology — move his right arm across his body — modern middle-class values — bend his right leg — merit as the arbiter of social and economic success — slowly move his bent leg over the other leg — the meritocratic principle in modern individualism — push the rest of his body over and pause — its two main arguments — slowly roll him back again — merit seen as a function of education and effort — straighten his right leg — merit as a function of breeding and innate intelligence and creativity — put his right arm by his side — the relationship between the philosophy of individualism and the concept of equality — straighten his head.

I often wondered how much of my college material Jonathan unconsciously absorbed along with the movements necessary for rolling over. What did go on inside the mind; inside a baby's mind? I wondered also about the two main arguments for the meritocratic principle. It was the old nature-nurture question in a modern, technological context, but now I also pondered the question subjectively, as an adoptive mother. How much of temperament and behaviour is genetically determined, and how much is due to upbringing? And just how important are a child's earliest experiences? I didn't know. But one thing I did know: Brian and I would make every effort to enhance Jonathan's natural abilities and compensate for those he had lost.

It took only a few weeks for Jonathan to roll over from left to right. Then, two months later, he rolled the other way. Brian and I were over the moon. He was only seven months, and he could roll over! Now we could think about teaching him to crawl. In the meantime, we persevered with another basic movement: getting him to open his clenched right hand. Frau Trepp-Jung had told us that the best way to encourage this was to stroke the back of his hand, and this we did constantly. At first it took half an hour before the muscles relaxed. Then, for a split second, his little fingers would spread wide before curling up again. And then we would start stroking all over again.

While working on Jonathan's tense muscles, we didn't forget his mind. We didn't want his poor little damaged brain to be filled only with my college material, with modern views of merit and success, but also with the unchanging principles of love and goodness. So we also combined physiotherapy with Bible reading, especially the Psalms. He might not have understood the words, but he enjoyed their rhythm and music. And, we believed, experienced their healing power.

I also sang to him all the children's hymns and choruses I could remember from my seventeen years as a Sunday School teacher, as well as nursery rhymes, snatches of opera, ballads, and German and Welsh folk songs. And, of course, we played music to him. He soon developed a preference for Verdi and Puccini. Or maybe he sensed my preference. But whatever the reason, a quick burst of "Libiamo" from *La Traviata* or "Che Gelida Manina" ("Your Tiny Hand is Frozen") from *La Boheme* quietened him in no time when he was tired or fractious.

As well as singing and playing music, I often danced with him. It was a spontaneous act on my part, because I love to dance, and because I loved hearing him giggle as I held him against my shoulder while I leapt and twirled around the room. But it also served the purpose of enhancing Jonathan's sense of rhythm, and creating in him a feeling for his own body and its relation to space.

Right from the start, before we knew that Jonathan had cerebral palsy, and before we had been told that he might be mentally retarded, we had been aware of how important it is to surround a new-born with light and colour and music and movement, and it had been natural for to us to talk to Jonathan constantly and point out things of interest, explain what things were, tell him what people were doing.... And right from the start we had kept plenty of toys within his reach; toys that he could touch, taste and smell, as well as see and hear.

The very first thing we had done, before Jonathan was born, was prepare an alcove in our bedroom for him, ensuring that it was bright, cheerful, and full of interest. My friend, Liz, and her husband had loaned us a beautiful Moses basket that fitted perfectly into the alcove, and their little daughter had loaned us her doll's bright red cover because, she said, Jonathan was a special baby and she wanted him to have the use of it for a while. She assured us that her doll wouldn't mind. The cover didn't match our décor, but who cared! It was a covering of love.

Over Jonathan's basket we had hung a butterfly mobile, and he loved to watch the vividly painted wings as the butterflies floated in lazy circles above his head. And on warm days, we carried him in his basket onto the end balcony, where he could look up into the canopied branches of the silver birch, and watch the sunlight playing on her green, fluttery leaves, and listen to them rustling in the breeze.

In spite of — or maybe because of — his brain damage, those first few months were happy, contented ones for all of us. But then, we had to take him to a neurologist for an electro-encephalogram (EEG) to check the electrical impulses in his brain. The poor little thing obviously couldn't understand why these cruel people were attaching great heavy weights to his head and wiring him to a huge machine, and he was terrified. He screamed, and screamed, and screamed, and there was nothing we could do to pacify him. The nursing staff was very patient, but because Jonathan's screaming affected the readings, the tests could not be carried out until he settled down.

Eventually, after two gruelling hours, he fell asleep, probably from sheer exhaustion, the tests were completed, and the neurologist confirmed what we already knew: that there was a huge gap in his brain on the left-hand side, running parallel with the lateral suture. The electrical impulses had to jump the gap, so there was an abnormal pattern; a pattern that often gives rise to epileptic fits.

The neurologist was reassuring. He told us that he knew of children with worse brain damage who never had fits. But, he warned us, there were others with far less damage who did. He gave us some valium pessaries to give to Jonathan if he had a prolonged convulsion, which could cause even more irreversible brain damage, and he told us to always carry them around with us. But when we got home and read the instructions, we discovered that they had to be kept refrigerated. What were we supposed to do? Carry the fridge around with us?

For weeks I was afraid to go out of the house, and my heart stopped if Jonathan so much as twitched. But in the end I decided that I couldn't carry on like that. I put the valium at the back of the fridge and tried to carry on life as normal. The pessaries remained there until they had passed their expiry date. And then we took them back to the chemist for disposal.

We didn't bother getting a repeat prescription. Just having the valium in the house had been a constant reminder that Jonathan might become epileptic, and we had other things to worry about. We would face that particular hurdle as and when we came to it. We also decided not to put Jonathan through the trauma of an EEG every six months, as the neurologist had recommended. There was nothing we could do if the gap widened — except stock up with more valium — so what was the point?

About the time Jonathan had his EEG, I read, in an autobiography written by the mother of a brain-damaged child, that parents of cerebral palsy children live with fear. We were discovering this to be horribly true. The fear was always there — fear and a persistent, gnawing ache. But we loved him. And because we loved him we could conquer fear, our own and Jonathan's. For, as we discovered when he was only a few days old, he too was afraid.

I knew from my midwifery and counselling experiences that a child is affected, for better or worse, by the mother's feelings towards it during pregnancy. I wasn't worried about Jonathan being permanently affected by Christine's rejection because, right from the moment of birth, he must have sensed that he was a very loved and wanted baby. And neither did I think that he would suffer any serious damage because of her turbulent relationship with her partner. So when, a week after his birth, he reacted with terror to the sound of raised, angry voices, I couldn't believe what I was witnessing.

We had switched on the TV, intending to watch a documentary, but the German soap that preceded it was still running, and two people were having a violent argument.

Suddenly, Jonathan gasped, went stiff, then began screaming as he writhed and kicked in his Moses basket. Brian and I both leapt for the TV to turn it off, and the moment it was silenced Jonathan stopped screaming and kicking. And when I picked him up, he gave a little shuddering sigh and buried his face in my shoulder.

Brian and I stared at each other, shocked and stunned, as I gently rubbed our baby's back. I was wondering if his reaction had been a coincidence; if he'd had an attack of colic just as we switched the TV on. But, Brian and I agreed, there had been no mistaking the look of terror on his face.

Over the next few weeks, we noticed that Jonathan always reacted strongly to the sound of raised voices or pop music, which plays a large part in many German commercials. But never did he react as violently as he had that first time, until a few days after the experience at the American consulate, when he had turned away from Christine and fixed his eyes on mine. We were watching the news when a film was shown of a street riot, with people fighting and shouting. We thought Jonathan was asleep. But suddenly he was wide awake, screaming with terror, his arm waving, legs kicking, his little face contorted with fear. Again, we leapt up to switch the TV off. And again, when I picked him up, he immediately calmed down.

Now we had no doubts. Jonathan was afraid. And we knew why. Christine had told me that she and her partner often had violent quarrels. And she had freely admitted that they some-times resorted to physical violence. She had once pulled a loaded gun on him. A baby in utero can hear voices, as well as sense its mother's feelings. And Christine's dominant feeling was anger. We had sensed anger in her from the beginning; she was like a smouldering volcano, in danger of erupting at any moment.

Christine had been badly abused and had a right to be angry. But she had let her anger turn to bitterness, and a desire for revenge. She had told me frankly that she was unwilling to forgive. Poor Christine! Tormented now, not by an abusive father and stepfather, but by her own rancour. And in tormenting herself she had also unintentionally hurt her unborn child.

When it dawned on Brian and me that Jonathan was afraid of Christine's voice, and of all loud, angry voices, I was thankful for the first time that my voice is a quiet one. I had often wished that it was less gentle and more forceful, but now I was glad that God had made my voice just the way it was. I was also glad that Christine had got her dates wrong and come to Germany sooner than she needed to.

Jonathan had been two weeks old when Frau Klammberg first came to see him, and she'd asked me if he responded to my voice.

"Yes," I'd replied. "He has done right from day one."

"Well, he has been used to your voice before he was born," she said smiling.

I started. Then, in dawning wonder, I smiled back at her. Of course he was used to my voice. He had heard it frequently during his final six weeks in that unwelcoming womb. It was a voice that he could hold onto: a voice that told him he was loved, and wanted and safe.

The last time Jonathan reacted with extreme fear, it was not to a voice but to loud pop music. It was when we were in England when he was eight weeks old. We had gone into a music shop to stock up with English videos, and as usual we couldn't concentrate because of the music blasting through the loud-speakers. The music was so loud that it got through to Jonathan, fast asleep in a front pack carried by his daddy. Brian told me later that he could feel the vibes coming from Jonathan. He was terrified, and even in his sleep he writhed and kicked. Of course, we left the shop immediately, and Jonathan promptly settled down, with his usual little shuddering sigh.

We didn't know the reason for Jonathan's fear of loud pop — loud classical music had no such effect — but we assumed that it had provided a background to Christine's violent fights. It would have been interesting to know, but the important thing was to help Jonathan overcome his fear. We did this through systematic desensitisation. At first, whenever there was pop music or raised, angry voices on the TV, we kept the picture on but turned the sound off, while we held Jonathan close and spoke reassuringly to him. Later, we left the sound on as well, but kept it very low. Then, over time, we increased the volume until it was within the normal range. Eventually, although Jonathan would always check to see if one of us was nearby, he no longer reacted with such blatant fear.

In spite of Jonathan's pre-birth fears, right from the beginning he radiated happiness and light, and at the Child Development Center he soon became known as The Sunshine Boy. The staff from other departments made a point of coming to see him when they were feeling frustrated and fed up. However whiny or cantankerous the other children were, Jonathan was guaranteed to give them a beaming smile and brighten their day.

Jonathan's smile was such a permanent fixture that when friends or relatives saw him looking serious, or frowning with concentration, they would comment, "Doesn't he look different."

And he did. He just didn't look himself unless his face was split in two by a huge grin. He was so contented that people even asked me on occasion, "Does he ever cry?"

Of course he cried. At times he kept us awake all night with his crying, because his feeding problems often resulted in severe colic. But it was on one of those nights that I discovered that I too had lost a fear; a fear that had never really gone away since the time we had Mark.

That night, Jonathan's colic was especially bad, and although we had given him the maximum number of antacid drops prescribed by the paediatrician, he continued to cry every time we laid him down. As long as someone was holding him upright and walking up and down the room with him, or rocking him in the rocking chair, he was alright. So Brian and I took it in turns to hold him, while the other tried to sleep.

Towards morning, I told Brian that I would take over because he had to go to work, whereas I, hopefully, could make up for my lack of sleep later in the day. So, for about five hours, from just before dawn until mid-morning, having already had a very disturbed night, I paced up and down the room with Jonathan over my shoulder.

By about ten-thirty I'd reached the end of my tether. I was dizzy with tiredness and sick with hunger. But if I put him down even for a moment, while I tried to get myself something to eat, he started screaming again. I decided I'd give him another half an hour then call the doctor. But during that half hour he fell asleep, and he stayed asleep even when I eased him into a more horizontal position. Just before he closed his eyes, he gave me a look that so clearly said, "Thank you, Mummy," that I was shaken into stunned wakefulness.

At the same moment, a powerful thought struck me: if this had happened ten years previously, when we'd had Mark, I might have ended up shaking or hitting him. Yet I'd had no desire to hit Jonathan: only the urge to comfort and console.

Then, as I looked down on my sleeping child, my tiredness and hunger seemed unimportant. I wanted to sit in that rocking chair forever, feeling that warm little body next to mine. And as he slept, and my mind wandered from Jonathan to Mark, to my own childhood and back again, it dawned on me that the urge to hit a child is a power issue.

When a child won't stop crying, parents tend to feel helpless, so they lash out. And in lashing out they regain a sense of power. But anyone can hit a child. All that needs is greater physical strength, and *all* parents have that. But to be able to soothe a child who is frightened, comfort a child who is upset and unhappy, take away a child's pain; that is real power. And it is the kind of power God demonstrates. It would be nothing for God to throw a few thunderbolts and wipe out the wicked: he's bigger than us. But he chooses instead to be patient, to soothe and comfort and heal, to win our love through loving. And in our ignorance, we call this power weakness!

Knowing that I held such tremendous power; that I could take away pain, wipe away tears, soothe away fear, was awe-inspiring and very humbling. I had been brought up in a home where fear was the dominant emotion. I had been full of fear and, like Christine, full of hate for my abusers — and for the world at large. Then, when I first came to the Lord at fourteen, I had asked God to teach me how to love.

I wondered now if Jonathan was part of the answer to that prayer. At one time I could never have loved a child who was less than perfect, but now I could love and accept Jonathan just as he was. And I was learning more and more through Jonathan what love is all about. But I was very far from being made perfect in love, and because of this I was not able to entirely cast out fear.

The fear that most haunted me — and Brian — was that the first neurologist's prognosis would prove correct: that Jonathan would never walk or use his right hand, that he'd be mentally retarded and epileptic. And the fear increased as the days and weeks passed in a blur of seemingly non-stop physio-therapy, and all he could do was roll over. There was no sign of him ever being able to move his limbs freely, or eat without being sick, or even make normal pre-speech sounds. And as the fears grew, we both became discouraged and depressed. And then, Brian had a strange experience that buoyed us up with new hope.

# Chapter 8

Brian was sitting at his drawing board at work, thinking about the seemingly endless physiotherapy and the very little it had accomplished, when he was startled by a series of vivid pictures flitting through his mind. Although a designer, Brian is not given to seeing mental images, and he knew at once that these pictures did not come from his own wishful thinking, but from God. In the first he saw Jonathan learning to walk, in the second he was in a field running and jumping, in the third he was sitting at a desk in school, and in the fourth he was at university.

When Brian told me about his experience, the depression I had been starting to feel suddenly lifted, and with new enthusiasm I renewed the task of teaching Jonathan the things that other babies do naturally: to crawl, sit up, use both hands.... I also regained the motivation to continue converting our study-cum-guestroom into a nursery. It was time for Jonathan to move into his own room.

The room was a large one, opening onto the side balcony, and as we still needed somewhere for guests, we left the bed settee and bedroom unit, but turned the integral desk into a changing area, exchanged the shelves of books for an assortment of toys and furry animals, and swapped the computer for a cot. And we papered one of the plain white walls with playful mice and nursery-rhyme shoe-houses, in colours that blended with the bright orange curtains.

Frau Trepp-Jung had recommended a beanbag chair, as this moulds itself to, and promotes awareness of, all parts of the body. So I made him one, and a matching duvet cover, with little orange and yellow trains chugging around little green hills. Then I did one thing more: I looked at the room from Jonathan's perspective. That is, from flat on the floor. This view was nowhere near as interesting, so I completed the room by pasting some pictures underneath the cot and desk — having first removed a few cobwebs. We were pleased with the end result. And more importantly, so was Jonathan.

I had first learned to actively see and experience things from a child's perspective during my training to assist with the swimming programme for handicapped children, when we first moved to Germany. One afternoon I had been hemiplegic, with one arm tied to my side and my legs tied together. I spent the entire afternoon trying to swim in straight lines, but instead going round in circles, while my legs kept sinking to the bottom. But the afternoon I most remembered was the one in which I was rendered blind.

I was blindfolded at the training centre, along with half of the trainees, and led by my seeing partner to the van waiting outside to transport us to the swimming pool. As we walked down the long corridor, we seemed to be going incredibly fast, and I had a persistent frightening sensation of something big and solid looming up in front of me. So I walked with my arm stretched forward to stop myself from walking into it. My partner assured me that there was nothing there, and that she would let me know if there was. And I believed her. But I still needed to keep my arm stretched forward. I realised then, perhaps for the first time, just how hard it was for me to put my complete trust in someone else.

My partner helped me up the steps into the van, then, amid a burst of laughter from the other occupants, she pulled me back, telling me that I was trying to stand on the seat. She got me sitting where I was supposed to be, fastened my seat belt, and we were off. It was strange travelling in complete darkness. I became much more aware of the movement of the van, and of sounds and sensations, and much less aware of time. I seemed to be in a time warp.

At the pool, my partner led me to a changing cubicle and left me to it. Although I had prepared everything before I became blind, I found myself fingering the seams of my swimsuit to make sure that it wasn't inside out. And before I emerged, I clumsily felt all around, on the seat, the shelf, and the floor, to make sure that I hadn't left anything, and I anxiously checked my swimsuit to make sure that it was covering everything that was supposed to be covered.

In the pool, I didn't know where I was, which direction I

85

was going in, or if I was about to collide with another swimmer or the side of the pool. So it was with great relief that I took off my blindfold at the end of the afternoon. And I appreciated so much more my own familiar world of light and colour.

My training and work with handicapped children helped me to identify with some of Jonathan's problems, especially his hemiplegia and disturbed vision: we weren't convinced that there was nothing wrong with his eyes. But I was still learning to tune into his feelings: to see and experience things as *he* saw and experienced them, and to recognise how the endless physio-therapy was affecting *him*.

We were now teaching Jonathan to crawl, going through a fresh series of movements, hour after hour, day after day, week in and week out, just as we had when teaching him to roll over. Then one day, I noticed that Jonathan was very twitchy, over-reacting to my slightest touch and to the smallest sound. I watched him anxiously, fearing that he was on the verge of his first epileptic fit. Then I noticed the strained look on his face, the wariness in his eyes, and the tenseness in his body, and I realised, to my utter amazement, that he was stressed out. In our attempts to encourage his brain to lay down new neural pathways, we had been overdoing it. We had been pushing him too far and too fast.

That evening, Brian and I discussed it, and we decided to give Jonathan a three-day break from physiotherapy, until his next visit to Frau Trepp-Jung's, to see what happened. The next day he seemed much more relaxed. And by the third day he was his normal, happy self again. So, when we resumed his physio-therapy, we worked harder at getting to know Jonathan — rather than getting the movements right — tuning into him and picking up his signals.

Soon, we had developed such a close relationship with our son that we knew just how far we could push him. And we knew when to stop. We also became acutely aware of timing: we knew when he was emotionally ready to learn a new skill. Much of the success of Jonathan's physiotherapy has been due to the fact that, whenever we began anything new, it was always at the optimum time.

But, there was one thing we couldn't let up on: his feeding. Jonathan had never been a plump baby, but now we could count his ribs. And the taller he got, the thinner he got. A childless old lady who lived downstairs used to ask me on occasion if I fed him. I was always tempted to reply, "No, it's cheaper this way. "

At least, now he was weaned, the awful choking sounds had stopped. But he continued to suffer from dysphagia: difficulty in swallowing. He dribbled constantly and had to wear a bib at all times to keep his clothes dry, and every meal took an age. So, eventually, he developed a preference for cold food. And, because eating was such an effort, he often became bored with the whole process, and gave up long before he was satisfied.

We found that it helped if we allowed him to watch a children's video while he ate, although later we had the difficult task of weaning him from that; he became convinced that meal-time was not family time, but Postman Pat or Thomas the Tank Engine time. We also tried giving him a little often. But even then, at least once a week, just as we were congratulating our-selves on having got a good meal down him, he would bring the whole lot back again.

Feeding was difficult and frustrating for us, and it must have been even more so for him. But, like all babies, Jonathan enjoyed experimenting with his food, and we egged him on as he made patterns with his finger in puréed vegetables, rubbed mashed potato through his hair, or banged his spoon in his pudding; although, once he'd discovered that food thrown across the room makes an interesting noise and a nice mess, we did put a stop to that particular experiment. Perhaps we allowed him to play around with his food more than we might have done because it was such a relief to see him doing and enjoying things that normal babies do and enjoy. And maybe it was also because *we* were learning to see patterns in food, and hear sounds of squelching and sloshing, splattering and plopping as if for the first time — as a baby would hear them.

At times it seemed that Jonathan enjoyed things more than is usual for young babies: from a very early age he had a well-developed sense of humour. And it was this, and one occasion in particular, that made me think very deeply about seeing and experiencing life from a different viewpoint. We had just arrived home after a session with the physiotherapist. It was cold outside, there was deep snow on the ground, and I was thinking that I could well understand why some German mothers swap their prams for sledges in the winter. My arms and back were aching from pushing Jonathan's pram up and down those steep hills, through snow that in places was flattened solid, in others rutted and ridged, and at the edge of the pavements, piled into feathery drifts.

As I walked through the front door, with Jonathan in my arms, I pushed back the hood of his snowsuit. Then, standing in front of the mirror on the hall wardrobe, I took off my own woolly hat. Some impulse made me put it on Jonathan's head, and as I did so, he looked at himself in the mirror and started to giggle.

I have always been a giggler myself, and if someone else starts, it's guaranteed to set me off. But when that someone else is a seven-month old baby with a mouth stretched so wide with laughter that it reaches the too-large hat flopping over his ears, and when I could feel the vibrations of erupting mirth from that little body in my arms, I didn't stand a chance. So there we stood, the two of us, convulsed with laughter while our reflections giggled and shook and hiccupped along with us.

Jonathan continued to giggle long after I had removed the hat and settled him in his baby seat in the living room, and I wondered just what was going on in that baby mind. Had he recognised the baby in the mirror as himself? Was it the sight of himself wearing *my* hat that had struck him as funny, the incongruity of it? Or did he think his reflection was a daft-looking stranger? I was pondering these questions as, grinning from ear to ear, I headed for the kitchen to make myself a drink.

As I waited for the kettle to boil, I remembered that time when, despairing of ever having a baby, I had come to the place where I could trust God, whatever he did to me; that time when it had been as if I'd stepped through a mirror and seen everything from a different perspective. And suddenly I wished that I could step through my hall mirror, push my way through the coats in the wardrobe, and find myself in a Narnia-like country: in another world where the snow had melted and it was eternal Spring.

I had often thought of my mind as a vast country confined within a small wardrobe-like skull: a place for hanging up thoughts and ideas. And I had often wondered if there was a door into that country that others could enter; if there were in fact many doors by which we could enter each other's inner worlds and find shared features and landscapes. And now, as I made my drink and carried it into the living room, I wondered yet again.

Jonathan was sitting there, gazing into the middle distance with a wide smile on his face, and at first he seemed unaware of my presence. Then he looked at me. And as we caught each other's eye he started to giggle again, while I choked and spluttered into my coffee. At that moment, I felt that we *had* found a door through a magic mirror into a shared world: a world of fun and laughter. God had truly made me to laugh. And what did it matter if our son couldn't crawl or sit up, or if his right arm hung uselessly at his side, if he couldn't swallow normally or see clearly, and if he still wasn't making normal baby sounds! In that inner world, where the great King reigned, Jonathan was perfect.

From that time, we began also to see a few outward changes. We now needed to stroke the back of Jonathan's hand for only five minutes before he opened it. And each time, his hand stayed open for longer. After another three months we needed only to tell him to "open fingers," and he would spread them wide, smiling proudly at his own cleverness. We could at last dispense with that particular exercise.

Jonathan also started to wriggle on his tummy, and by swinging himself from side to side, he was able to move forward a few centimetres. It wasn't much. But it was the start of his journey towards independence. We now spent hours holding a toy in front of him, then moving it just out of reach as he stretched his good arm towards it, to encourage him to keep wriggling forward. It was difficult knowing how far to go with this. We didn't want to tease him: to end up discouraging instead of assisting. And my mind went back to the time when it had seemed that God was teasing us with the held-out promise of a baby. Had he been encouraging us to reach out, to move forward, to discover new potential in ourselves? I didn't know. But during this period of Jonathan's development, I did a lot of thinking.

Jonathan was certainly discovering *his* potential. Except in one area. Here there was no sign of any development at all, and a fear that had lain dormant ever since the brain scan, when he was three months old, now began to awaken. The scan had shown that Broca's area, the part of the brain concerned with speech, was damaged, and we were afraid that Jonathan would never talk. We knew, of course, that it isn't just the left side of the brain that controls speech; the right side — Jonathan's undamaged side — also plays a part. But as he neared his first birthday and still wasn't making any of the normal pre-speech sounds, the fear could no longer be ignored.

Several times in the past, Dr Lieb had commented on Jonathan's retarded speech, but he had agreed with us that Jonathan had enough to contend with without also having to cope with pre-speech therapy. Now, however, we decided that after our holiday we would go back to the paediatrician and ask him what this therapy entailed, and maybe consider going ahead with it.

Jonathan was eleven months old when we set off for our first real holiday since his birth. We had rented an apartment by Lake Titisee in the Black Forest, having decided that a self-catering holiday would be the most practical with a baby. We were driving down the autobahn when, suddenly, from the back of the car, we heard an unmistakeable, "Ba-ba-ba-ba."

I spun round, and Jonathan beamed at me, while he said again, "Ba-ba-ba-ba."

My face wreathed in smiles, I repeated it back to him, and Jonathan squirmed with delight, his entire body showing his pleasure. Then, obviously thinking that this was a wonderful new game, he gave a little chuckle, pursed his lips and, with intense concentration, said yet again, "Ba-ba-ba-ba."

Overwhelmed with joy and relief, I now laughed aloud as

I repeated once more, "Ba-ba-ba-ba."

"Ba-ba-ba-ba," laughed Jonathan.

And now, having finished overtaking a string of Dutch caravans, Brian too joined in: "Ba-ba-ba-ba."

And all the way to our destination, the three of us were laughing and chuckling and saying over and over, "Ba-ba-ba-ba."

It was the most beautiful sound in the world.

It was while we were in the Black Forest that Jonathan, for the first time, reached out for a toy with his right hand. And it was there, in the holiday apartment, that he perfected his wriggling technique. It wasn't crawling by any means, but he was able to move, slowly and laboriously, the length of his own body. His world was expanding.

Jonathan loved every minute of the holiday, his blue eyes wide as he took everything in, his ears alert to every sound. He had recently discovered bouncing and, as we supported him in a standing position, he bounced as we sat on the grass, feeding the ducks or inquisitive sparrows. He bounced as we perched on piled-up logs in the forest, watching red squirrels at play. He bounced as we rested on wooden benches in the town square, looking at the colourful shops full of cuckoo clocks and dirndl skirts and carved wooden nutcrackers. He bounced throughout an entire boat ride on the green-fringed lake, and on the train, all the way to Freiburg. He bounced, in spite of our endeavours to keep him still, as we glided on ski lifts up silent, pine-clad mountains. And not content with that, he bounced on his bottom as he sat in his stroller in open-air cafes, eating Black Forest Gateau and watching the world go by.

Maybe it was the extra stimulation the holiday provided. Or the bouncing. Or maybe he just wanted to say thank you for a wonderful time. Whatever the reason, two weeks after our return to Wehen, and just before his first birthday, he did something I will never forget. He hugged me with two arms. It took several attempts to get his stiff right arm onto my shoulder, and in the process my face got thumped and my eye scratched. But no mother, I am sure, revelled in her child's embrace as much as I did when he finally succeeded.

We had a little party for Jonathan's birthday. Our guests were a young couple with a ten-month old baby called Daniel, and a missionary friend we had known in England. Brian had just bought a video camera, and on this special day he made full use of his new "toy", recording the babies playing on the floor or bouncing on knees to a new nursery rhyme tape, the walk in the forest, and the birthday tea, complete with jelly and ice cream and a cake with one candle. It was while he was filming that Daniel's mother turned to me and asked blithely, "Well, Jenny, how was your year?"

I felt a surge of annoyance. How could she be so insensitive, so lacking in empathy? Couldn't she even begin to imagine what the year had been like for us, to see it from our perspective: the joy of the birth; the initial fear that Jonathan might be blind; that terrible visit to the neurologist and the picture of black emptiness; the anger, the grief that followed; the stress of the EEG; the endless physiotherapy.... And to ask such a question while my answer was being recorded!

But then, how could she understand? She was young; she had a vibrant, exciting personality that had seemingly never been touched by tragedy; and she had a big, healthy boy who hadn't given her a moment's anxiety, who had done all the right things at the right time — or earlier. And we had told her very little of our heartache and suffering. We had focused on the positive, sharing with her and her husband mainly the things we had in common: a love of Jesus and the wonder and excitement of having a new baby.

I pretended that I hadn't heard her question, and continued spooning birthday cake into Jonathan's smiling mouth. But she persisted, her voice loud and eager, "How was your year, Jenny?"

I smiled at her, shrugged, and said, "Hectic!" What else could I say?

When the party was over, I asked myself the same question. How was my year? And I answered: It was wonderful. It was terrible. It was a lot of fun. It was sheer hard work. It was a dream come true. It was a nightmare. And all this for a child who was not yet legally ours, who didn't even have the same nationality as us. We had hoped that the adoption would be finalised before his first birthday, but legal wheels turn slowly. And until the adoption was finalised, we couldn't apply for him to be naturalised as a British citizen.

Daniel's mother not only had a healthy child who didn't need constant visits to the physiotherapist, the paediatrician, the ophthalmist, the optometrist, the orthopaedic surgeon and the neurologist; she had a child she could take through customs without having to produce a letter of authorisation from Social Services.

Now that Jonathan's physiotherapy was getting easier, and he was starting, at last, to make normal baby sounds, my anxiety about the adoption was coming to the fore. How much longer would it be? Would it all go smoothly? Or were there yet more storms ahead?

# Chapter 9

The weeks passed, and still there was no word of the adoption. Frau Klammberg had assured us that everything was going through the system, so all we could do was wait. In the meantime, we persevered with Jonathan's physiotherapy. It was becoming easier, partly because he didn't need so much of it, but also because he could now follow verbal instructions and carry out the exercises himself. On the down side, this made it mentally wearing as we had to constantly remind him to open his fingers, or put his right arm forward as he wriggled across the room. But especially wearing was teaching him new skills, the latest being climbing up onto the settee:

"Put your left arm on the seat. Now lift your right arm. Your right arm, Darling. Won't it go? Oh, nearly! Try again. Come on, keep trying. That's it! Well done! Now, can you put it down on the seat? Oops! That was a bit of crash landing, wasn't it? (Giggles from Jonathan.) Now, turn your hand over. Turn it over, Darling. Like this. Won't it go? Never mind. Mummy will help you with that bit. Now, open your fingers. Good boy! Now bend your left knee. That's it. Now put your left foot flat on the floor. Oops! Your hand's fallen down. Let's do that bit again...."
So many times, I wanted to put my hand under his little bottom and push him up onto the settee. But I usually resisted the temptation, at least until the moment when I felt he'd had enough.

Now that he was getting older, we were also able to incorporate physiotherapy with play, or turn it into play. And this too made it easier. Jonathan loved being a steam engine while I provided counter-resistance to his piston-legs, or being a racing car while I swung his stretched-out legs around imaginary bends. Often he would end up giggling helplessly as the car crashed and he rolled over and over on the carpet-track. And of course, I would join in. Jonathan's giggles were very infectious.

It was strange that Jonathan's brain damage, that had caused so much worry and fear, was also the cause of so much fun and laughter. Or was it the other way round? Perhaps the strangeness lay in its being a source of unhappiness. I thought back to the time when I had been a home missions worker in Aberdeen. There was a town nearby that I loved to visit on my days off, and there was one vantage point that I especially loved. From there I could see the entire granite-grey town nestling among the hills, and a headland with an ancient castle jutting out into the sea, with seagulls constantly circling, their raucous cries mingling with the whoosh and shush of waves sweeping the shingle. It was a beautiful view, spoiled only by one thing. Right in the centre of my line of vision was an enormous gasholder.

Why is it, I thought, that the most beautiful views, the most wonderful experiences, the loveliest of people have something to spoil them: some monstrosity that cannot be overlooked rising up in the middle? I could not ignore Jonathan's handicap. It intruded, like the gasworks, into a scene of love and laughter. But maybe it was because of the gasworks that I appreciated so much, and learned to focus on, the surrounding beauty.

The love and laughter, the constant giggles, were most in evidence as we tried to instil in Jonathan a sense of balance. We had bought him a push-along horse for his birthday that could also be used as a rocking horse. And it was as a rocking horse that it was most used in the first few months, even though he couldn't sit on it unsupported. If we let go, just for a second, he fell off. It reminded me of my school days in the gym. I was useless at PE, and especially hated the vaulting horse. I invariably fell off sideways, and the poor gym teacher used to stand there, waiting to catch me, never knowing which side I'd fall off next. With Jonathan it was easier. He always fell off to the left.

In order to help his sense of balance, Frau Trepp-Jung had recommended that we buy a rocking chair, and Jonathan loved to sit on my knee while I rocked and sang nursery rhymes. His favourites were "Rock-a-bye-baby", "This is the way the farmer rides", and "I'm the king of the castle", all of which involved pushing him off my knee and catching him as he pitched backwards. He would wait in fearful excitement for the moment when he fell from the tree top, or into the ditch, or down from the castle, then squeal with delight as I swept him up again, his face a picture of merriment as he bounced exuberantly in my arms.

As well as a rocking chair, Frau Trepp-Jung had also recommended a large, gymnastics ball, which we used to lay or sit him on while gently rolling him from side to side. He giggled whenever he started to slide or lurch forward, and thought it especially funny if I had to make a grab for him. It obviously never entered his head that I might actually drop him.

If only we could have learned that simple, child-like trust in God. We believed that God wouldn't drop us, that the adoption would be finalised without a hitch, but we could never entirely free ourselves from the question, "But what if...?"

In a sense, we had more faith in Frau Klammberg, even though she couldn't speak or understand our language and had required an interpreter; and had needed help from International Social Services to make sure that Christine took the right bits of paper to the right places. As she once said, laughing, "Next time I have a British couple wanting to adopt an American baby, I will know what to do."

The letter from the magistrate's court finally arrived on October 16th 1990, when Jonathan was fourteen months old. We had expected a certificate of some kind, so when the registered letter arrived by the afternoon post, I wasn't sure if this was it. My hands were trembling as I tore open the envelope and skip-read the letter. The gist of it seemed to be that the adoption had been approved. But I wasn't sure. I hadn't understood a lot of it. I now re-read the last paragraph. It was to the effect that Jonathan could use our surname. But when? Was this just a preliminary notice, or was it the long-awaited finalisation?

I now began reading the letter thoroughly, checking out every unfamiliar word in our German-English dictionary, an enormous volume containing over 200,000 words and phrases. But many of the words weren't in the dictionary, and I started to panic. And the more I panicked, the less I understood. Then I realised that I didn't even know what the heading, a word written in big letters, meant.

My hands were now shaking quite badly, and my eyes

were blurred as I thumbed through the dictionary. At last I found the word I wanted, and I looked at the English translation. It meant — rejected. My heart seemed to stop, and my mind went numb, refusing to accept it. It couldn't be. God wouldn't take Jonathan away from us. He wouldn't let them do that. Not after bringing us so far.

Although part of me had shut down and nothing was registering, another part, deep inside, was screaming, "No, God, please — not that!"

Yet another part of me was being very practical and down-to-earth, and calmly telling me to read the letter again. The third reading confirmed that the gist of the letter was favourable, and that the last paragraph definitely said something about Jonathan using our surname. But how could that be if our application had been rejected? It didn't make sense.

At last I phoned Brian at work, saying only that a registered letter had arrived from the judge's office, and that I couldn't understand it. It was now mid-afternoon and, since Brian worked flexitime, he packed up early and came straight home. It was about half an hour's drive from his workplace, and by the time he arrived, I was fluctuating between mild euphoria and a numb despair.

Brian read the letter, and as he perused it, I watched a frown gather and deepen on his brow. "I don't understand it either," he said at last. "But it seems to be okay."

"It's that word there," I said, pointing to the heading. "It means rejected."

"It can't!" said Brian. "Are you sure?"

"Yes," I replied. "See for yourself." And I pointed to the word in the dictionary.

Brian looked at it, and his frown settled into a seemingly permanent fixture. A few minutes passed as we both stood there, battling with our own private thoughts. Suddenly, Brian glanced across at the letter, then at the word in the dictionary, then he looked at me. "You great ninny!" he laughed. "You've looked up the wrong word!"

I now checked the word in the letter again, and the one in the dictionary, then I started to laugh as relief flooded over me. The word in the letter was "ausgesprochen", meaning proclamation. I should have known it. It was merely the past tense of "aussprechen" — to speak out — a word I had known since my schooldays. The word I had looked up in the dictionary was "ausgeschlossen", the past tense of "ausschliessen"— to shut out, or reject.

We stood there a few minutes more, laughing at our mistake and enjoying our relief, trying to take it all in. Then we phoned Frau Klammberg to ask her if she could explain the letter to us. But she wasn't there. And neither was her assistant, Herr Schatten. So there was nothing for it but to wait until the next morning and ask the physiotherapist. For some unknown reason, we didn't want to ask any of our German neighbours.

The next morning, having explained our difficulty, I handed the letter to Frau Trepp-Jung. She first gave Jonathan some bricks to play with, then perched cross-legged on a table to read it. As I waited, my gaze wandered from the physiotherapist, with her short, chic hairstyle and sloppy jersey with the wide, horizontal black stripes, to the equipment in the large hall — the big, square swing and the hammock hanging from the rafters, the green nets draped over the gallery rail, the climbing frames on the wall, and on the floor a long red tunnel and a line of trays with different substances for walking on: sand, pebbles, wood chips, fur and crinkly wool, possibly unpicked from another of her sloppy jerseys.

She finished the letter, then read it again. And again. "It is written in archaic German," she told me at last. "I do not understand many of the words because they are no longer in current use. But yes, it is what you are waiting for. Jonathan is now legally yours."

I let out a great sigh, not only of relief that the adoption had been finalised at last, but because I now knew why we'd had so much difficulty understanding the letter. If a German couldn't understand it, what chance did we have? "But what about him using our surname?" I asked. "Can we change his name now, or do we have to wait for some other document?"

She read the last paragraph again. "You may change

it now," she told me. "Yes, I think that is so." Then, giving Jonathan a hug and shaking my hand, she gave us her heart-felt congratulations.

And now, congratulations began to pour in as we shared the good news with our relatives and friends. We were touched by the number of people — our German neighbours, British expatriates, and American friends at church and work — who said how lucky Jonathan was to have us. And one response was especially affecting. We had taken Jonathan to the paediatrician for a routine check, and while he lay on the examination table, gurgling and cooing at the fairy-tale characters painted on the wall, I told Dr Lieb that the adoption had been finalised, and that Jonathan now had our name. I expected the doctor to shake our hands and congratulate *us*. Instead, with a beaming smile, he turned to Jonathan, gave *his* hand a hearty shake, and congratulated *him*.

With the steady flow of congratulations and best wishes, that came by letter and card as well as verbally, came a growing sense of quiet joy; a joy that we hugged to ourselves and that showed itself only in sudden, involuntary smiles and occasional bursts of song. We had expected that, as soon as we heard from the judge's office, we would want to go out and celebrate. But after such a long wait, and with all the stress and anxiety the letter had aroused, we didn't feel like celebrating. Like the day we had first signed, committing ourselves to adopting Jonathan while fighting back tears of grief, the reality had failed to live up to the fantasy: it was the beautiful view spoiled by a gasholder. But it didn't matter. As the days and weeks passed, the joy became all-pervasive, the stress and anxiety was forgotten. We were safe. No one could take Jonathan from us now, as they had Mark. The future looked beautiful.

With the increasing joy and sense of security came an increasing desire to give Jonathan back to God. Brian and I had believed, from the very moment we knew of his existence, that he was in God's hands, and we had dedicated him to God in our hearts. But now we could dedicate him publicly.

I had often dreamed of taking a brand new baby to church, dressed in a beautiful long christening gown, while our families proudly looked on. And I had thought of various people I would like as godparents. But when Jonathan was born and our chaplain had asked if we would like to have him dedicated, I had explained that I didn't feel we could while he was just a foster child. We would wait until the adoption was finalised. I hadn't thought it would take so long.

Naturally, now that we could go ahead with the ceremony, we wanted to arrange a day when as many relatives and friends as possible could be there. We discussed it with our chaplain and discovered that he was away until after Christmas. Then there were field exercises and other military duties, so the earliest date he could suggest was February 18th.

We didn't think this would be a good time for travelling as we often had deep snow in February, so we suggested putting it off until Easter. In one respect, this would be ideal because our friend, Pam, whom we wanted as a godmother, had already planned to stay with us then, as she did every Easter. But then, the dedication would clash with Easter services. So February 18th it had to be. Jonathan would then be eighteen months.

We immediately invited Brian's parents. But they were both approaching eighty, and not in the best of health, so they didn't want to face the long journey. We were sad about this, and I found myself wishing that my own parents were alive, and that they could be there with us, even though they had never wanted me. I especially missed having a mother. I had been thinking of her more since Jonathan's birth, and for the first time wondering about the real mother: the fun-loving, musical, creative mother I had occasionally caught glimpses of but never really known. But there was no point dwelling on this. They were dead. So, my thoughts turned to other relatives.

And now we discovered that, for various reasons, none of the relatives could come. So that just left friends. We knew that, as a teacher, Pam wouldn't be able to get away mid-term, and recently a group of American friends had returned to the US. So, we ended up with just inviting the chaplain and his wife, Daniel's parents, and four other couples whom we had only just met.

The day arrived, and I dressed Jonathan, not in a long, white christening gown, but in a little pair of navy trousers and a waistcoat with a pattern of red rosebuds. He looked lovely, and as we placed his baby seat as usual in the church aisle, he beamed and cooed at everyone, raising smiles on many faces. We had been disappointed that we hadn't been asked to choose a hymn or Bible reading, and now, as we looked through the order of service, we were concerned to find no mention of the dedication. The chaplain, although a high-ranking and efficient officer, was notoriously absent-minded, and we wondered if he had forgotten. But, no. He hadn't forgotten the dedication. He had just forgotten to inform his secretary.

The service began with a reading from Psalm 150. But as I listened to those familiar and loved words of praise, with the conclusion, "Let everything that has breath praise the Lord", I realised that I was feeling very deflated, tearful almost, and certainly not in the mood for praising. Then I glanced across at Jonathan. He grinned at me and tried to clap his hands, his left hand as usual not quite connecting with the right, which he held stiffly in front of him. I smiled back at him, and it struck me that, in his own way, Jonathan was praising the Lord. He was celebrating life: he was always full of wonder and excitement and enthusiasm. And his love of life rubbed off on all he came in contact with — as it did now with me. Yes, I could praise the Lord, in spite of all the disappointments.

The dedication began, and as the chaplain, a tall, thin man, held Jonathan in his arms, he said, "This is a very special child."

"Ga-ga," said Jonathan, making his latest sound, and smiles rippled through the congregation like waves of liquid praise.

With amazing aplomb, the chaplain continued, saying that Jonathan had astounded doctors with his progress, and he repeated what the neurologist had said: that Jonathan would probably never walk or use his right side, that he might be mentally retarded, and that he would most likely be epileptic. I was surprised to see the smiles broaden and turned to look at Jonathan. Then I bit my lip to stifle a giggle. He was peering intently into the chaplain's face, their noses almost touching.

The chaplain went on in his usual laid-back manner, saying how lucky Jonathan was to have such loving and dedicated parents. Jonathan nodded, and there were a few suppressed titters of laughter. I fixed my gaze at some spot on the far wall, not daring to look at Jonathan again, or at anyone else. I knew that my urge to giggle was partly due to embarrassment. I hadn't expected such praise of us.

And now, the chaplain got to the part of the service where he asked the congregation if they would join with us, and support us, as we brought Jonathan up in the Christian faith. It struck me as strange, and sad, that in another three years not one of those people would be there. They would all have been posted to other parts of the world. And where would *we* be? Who would there be to help and support us then?

The theme of the service had been God as our Rock, unchanging and unmoving. Being a member of a military church, where there was such a rapid turnover, made one very aware of change, of endings and beginnings, and perhaps more reliant on God and more appreciative of his unchangeableness. The congregation promised — for the time being — to help us raise Jonathan as a Christian. The chaplain prayed. Then he handed Jonathan back to us. It was over.

We left the church with very mixed feelings. We had gone ahead of our guests to put the last-minute touches to the buffet lunch, and on the journey home both of us were feeling happy and disappointed at the same time. God has made me to laugh, I thought, and all who hear will laugh with me. Jonathan had certainly made everyone else laugh. But the laughter for us was again tinged with sadness.

To add to our disappointment, two of the invited couples didn't turn up. One couple had apologised earlier: they had another appointment out of town. Another couple simply forgot. We had a pleasant afternoon, but at first it was lacking the party spirit. The only real animation came from Daniel, who was running around chattering nineteen to the dozen, while Jonathan lay on his back and said, "Ga-ga."

But Jonathan had a few party tricks he was keeping

in reserve. And later, he demonstrated how he could climb onto the settee all by himself, and how he could crawl, no longer wriggling on his tummy but, stiffly and awkwardly, shuffling along on his hands and knees. But it was his third party trick that really got things going. He was starting to sit up.

Jonathan had started to sit up two months earlier, but he still hadn't perfected the technique. Now, as usual, he lay on his back and jerked his body from side to side until he found himself sitting, very precariously, on his little padded bottom: he was wearing a nappy under his new, navy trousers. Then, as usual, his right leg slowly lifted into the air as if pulled by an invisible string, and just as slowly he toppled over to the side, to shouts of "Timber!" from his daddy and me which, as always, sent him off into fits of giggles.

As at the dedication service, ripples of laughter spread around the room. And the laughter increased as, over and over, Jonathan jerked himself into a sitting position, beamed proudly at everyone, then fell to the side as his right leg involuntarily lifted into the air, his little body heaving and shaking with erupting mirth.


It would have been nice if we could have finished the day with the memory of Jonathan's giggles. Instead, it ended on a note of embarrassment and anger. I had told the chaplain and his wife about the study we had converted into a nursery, and they wanted to see it. I was pleased at their interest, and proudly opened the door into the blue and orange room with its playful mice and little toy trains puffing around little green hills. Immediately, I was hit by a smell that was so obnoxious and overpowering that I almost gagged, and I rushed to the window to open it, in spite of its being a cold February day. I apologised, explaining that Daniel's mum had just been in, changing his nappy. They pretended not to notice the smell, and looked around the room with interest. But they didn't stay long.

When everyone had left, I looked at Jonathan's changing mat. It was smeared with faeces, and angrily I got out some disinfectant to clean it. But the smell remained. And when I shut the window, to allow the room to warm up before putting Jonathan to bed, it got steadily worse. Later, as I lay Jonathan in his cot, we wondered again about his sense of smell, and how he could bear to stay in that room. We certainly couldn't have. We could barely stay long enough to go through his little bedtime prayer ritual. But Jonathan seemed totally unaffected.

The next day I cleaned the mat again, with yet more disinfectant, this time washing underneath the mat and all the surrounding area. But nothing would shift that terrible stink. It was two days later when I found an unwrapped nappy oozing liquid faeces placed in a pretty Japanese waste-paper basket I'd had when I was in missionary work in Aberdeen, and had left in our old study for Jonathan to play with.

I felt especially angry and upset that this had become the dominant memory of a day that, from beginning to end, had been full of disappointments. I thought wryly, this was the gasworks with a vengeance. But, as I contemplated that scene in Scotland with the grey, granite town, the ancient castle on the headland, the sea washing onto a shingle beach, and the circling seagulls, I realised that it was the view, and the sound and smell of the sea, which had remained most firmly fixed in my mind. Not the gas-holder. And it would be the sight of Jonathan's beaming smiles and inquisitive stares, and the sound of his giggles that, in time, would become the dominant memory of this special day.

And now there were two more special days coming up: my first Mother's Day since the adoption was finalised, and in May, my graduation. Would these too consist of giggles and gasworks? I hoped not. I had waited a very long time to be a mother, and longer still to obtain a university degree. I had wanted to go to university when I left school, but my father hadn't allowed me to, saying that I was only a girl and girls were too stupid to learn.

Mother's Day and Graduation Day would commemorate the realisation of two dreams that, in this past year, had become intertwined. I desperately wanted them to be unspoiled, especially as we also had two doctors' appointments coming up: first with the ophthalmist, who was giving us conflicting reports about Jonathan's eyes, and then with the paediatrician, who wanted to discuss his retarded speech. But maybe I was asking too much.

# Chapter 10

We went to the ophthalmist with our usual feelings of apprehension, wondering what he would discover this time. He had tested Jonathan's eyes at each visit, and each time the result was different. On the previous visit, he had told us that, although the vision in Jonathan's left eye was very poor, there did seem to be some improvement. Yet the time before, he had explained, in medical jargon, that the optic nerve supplying the left eye was atrophying from lack of use because the brain wasn't interpreting the visual messages. He had also explained that, although left hemisphere brain damage, as in Jonathan's case, affects the right side of the body, it is the left eye that is affected, because the optic nerves cross over.

Now, there was the usual tense wait while the ophthalmist went through his repertoire of tests. Then he told us, with a smile, that there was no change. We felt relieved but confused, as this didn't stack up with our own observations. We had long ago graduated from "Peep-bo" games, which had invariably sent Jonathan into fits of giggles, to "What-can-you-see-with-your-left-eye?" games. And Jonathan didn't like these games at all. He became disorientated and upset when we tried covering his right eye, and he would try to pull our hand away, or duck his head to look underneath it. We wondered if he was seeing very much at all with his left eye. But there were other things to worry about. So, for the time being, we accepted the ophthalmist's findings.

We now saw the optometrist who told us, as before, that Jonathan's squint could be corrected by surgery, although the operation would be complicated by his having an upward as well as an outward squint. And again she warned us that the squint could return, and that subsequent operations were usually less successful. Brian and I had discussed this, and we told her that we had decided to put off surgery until the squint bothered Jonathan. It had long stopped bothering us.

Some weeks later we saw the paediatrician about

Jonathan's delayed speech, and he suggested again that we take him for pre-speech therapy. We now asked Dr Lieb what this entailed, and he explained that Jonathan would be encouraged to produce sounds from a variety of musical instruments, and to repeat sounds made by the therapist. We told him that Jonathan was already doing this: we let him play on our keyboard and strum our guitars; he had a toy drum, bells, a shaker, xylophone, and a mouth organ; and when my head could stand it, we even let him bang saucepan lids. And there was no end to the variety of sounds *we* made at him. Besides, we were hopeful that he would start talking when he no longer needed to concentrate on learning to walk. Dr Lieb agreed, and now suggested that we reviewed his need for therapy in another six months. We left his surgery feeling discouraged at the thought of yet more seemingly endless repetition, but also pleased to know that, from the earliest days, we had been doing all the right things.

Jonathan was certainly receiving many different kinds of stimulation, both at the American Child Care Center, where he continued to be a favourite, and at home. Most weekends we took him on trips, usually to one of the villages on the Rhine, and we often went shopping in one or other of our three local cities, Wiesbaden, Mainz and Frankfurt. We walked for miles in the hills and forests, and we took him to zoos, museums and art galleries. It was funny watching Jonathan's reactions to the paintings.He would turn away in seeming disgust from a Picasso, look in bewilderment at a Miró, screw his face up at a Van Gogh, and point, laughing, at the bright colours of a Kandinsky or Macke. What a pity, we thought, that he couldn't talk and explain his reactions and opinions. And it was a pity too that he wouldn't remember any of these excursions. I often wondered what his first memory would be.

I now began thinking a lot about my own first memory. I was four and standing outside a maternity hospital with my father and brother. My mother was in an upstairs window, a pink shawl around her shoulders and her blonde hair a shining halo of light in the evening sun. She saw us and waved, and we all waved back. She had just given premature birth to my sister, Lynn, who had died. Whistler's painting of his mother always brought this scene back to me, possibly because of the way she was sitting. I hoped Jonathan's first memory would be a happier one.

But now it was Mother's Day, and I was about to create a happy memory — for myself at least. For the first time since the adoption was finalised, I could be part of that day, because now I was a mother. For over fourteen years I had hated Mother's Day. But there was one in particular I would never forget.

We had begun attending a military church in Wiesbaden, and our pastor, a missionary, was on furlough in the US. His temporary replacement, a military chaplain, had hit on the idea of gathering the children at the front and having them call their mothers out, one by one, to present them with posies of flowers. The ceremony would end with all the children and their mothers grouped together, while he prayed for them. The idea worked well, except for one thing: at the end, there was only one woman left sitting in the congregation — me.

The chaplain suddenly realised what he had done, and he called me out too. If he had simply made some comment about my being a mother in Israel — even if he hadn't meant it — and given me a posy from the ones left over, all would have been well. But, no. He began to apologise profusely, saying how terribly sorry he was, that he hadn't done it deliberately, that he just hadn't thought.

I was willing him to shut up, and a friend, having glimpsed my face, began surreptitiously shaking her head at him, mouthing for him to carry on with the service. But he took not the slightest notice.

"I really didn't mean to leave you out," he said again. "I just didn't think when I arranged for all the mothers to come to the front that there would be anyone who wasn't a mother. I'm really very sorry."

I was now in tears, but as the mothers and their children were huddled in a group, rather than lined up facing the front, I was able to turn my face from the congregation without its being obvious why.

"I knew there wouldn't be any singles here today," he continued. "They're all out in the field. And you just don't expect an older married woman not to have children."

The tears were now streaming down my face, and as my friend put her arm around me, I buried my face in her shoulder. This seemingly got through to the chaplain because he came to a sudden stop. Then he asked the congregation to rise while he prayed for the mothers — and me. I decided then that I would never go to another Mother's Day Service until I had a child of my own.

And now I had a child of my own. I dressed him in the little navy suit with the red rosebuds that he'd worn for his dedication, and afterwards we photographed him holding the single red carnation — the flower of choice for that year — that he had presented to me during the service. But I didn't need a photograph to remind me of that day. It was printed indelibly on my mind. It was the day I felt normal, like everyone else, taking part in a simple ritual that acknowledged, not only the importance of the Mother Church, but the great value God places on human mothers.

That red carnation became a symbol for me of the wonder and beauty of motherhood. Being a mother has its pains, and didn't I know it! But there were times, like today, when being a mother was pure, unadulterated joy.

There were also times — many times — when Jonathan was a little bundle of joy, a child with a special gift of spreading happiness wherever he went. But he was also becoming very demanding, wanting us to turn the pages of a book, hold paper for him while he cut it or crayoned, hold a duplo brick while he slotted in another piece, hold his plastic train while he hooked the carriage on. His having only one hand was frustrating for all of us. But we were learning to be inventive, and with a little imagination and a few gadgets — clipboards, weights, and Brian's cardboard and wire creations — we were able to help Jonathan become more independent.

At times Jonathan was too independent; he had a definite mind of his own. But he also wanted very much to please, and he hated being disapproved of. Although Jonathan had "inherited"

Brian's sweet temper, the combination of stubbornness and sensitivity he had "inherited" from me could at times be explosive, as we were discovering more and more. He became upset and tense if he couldn't achieve what he set out to do, or if he sensed our disapproval or annoyance, and the more tense he got, the more handicapped he became, which made him tense all the more. Reassuring Jonathan and helping him calm down when he was in one of his strops, so that he could function physically, was for Brian and me a never ending and thankless task.

Frau Trepp-Jung was now regularly experiencing Jonathan's strong-mindedness. During the twice weekly hour-long sessions, there was no time to spend persuading him to do something he didn't want to do. So, if Frau Trepp-Jung wanted him to lie in a hammock, feeling the movement and seeing the world through mesh, she would ask him to crawl through the tunnel. Sure enough, Jonathan would refuse to cooperate until she lifted him, writhing and kicking, into the hammock. Then, with a look of triumph, he would lie back and gaze at the room swinging gently to and fro, while Frau Trepp-Jung and I exchanged knowing smiles.

The neurologist had said that Jonathan might be mentally retarded. We had never really believed that. Even as a baby we could see the intelligence in his eyes. And even then, there was a strength about him. Now, his ability to think, to work things out and make his own decisions, was proving that, far from being retarded, he was very bright. This was confirmed on one of those many occasions when Jonathan wanted his own way.

When he started crawling at eighteen months, we child-proofed the house: we moved all our heavy or breakable ornaments to the top shelves, covered the plug sockets, and put a gate at the kitchen entrance. Then, with a very few exceptions, we let Jonathan go where he wanted and do what he wanted. It didn't take him long to discover an exception. He discovered how to turn the TV on. I was in the kitchen at the time, and when I heard voices, I went into the living room, switched the TV off and, smiling at Jonathan, said, "Don't turn the TV on, Darling, there's a good boy."

109

I returned to the kitchen, and a few minutes later, on it came again. Once more I turned it off, this time shaking my head and saying firmly, "No, Jonathan. That's naughty. "

The same thing happened a third time, but I persisted, telling him yet again that this was not allowed. But Jonathan could be persistent too. He turned it on a fourth time. And for the fourth time I told him, "No, Jonathan. That's naughty."

And now, Jonathan stared back at me, his big blue eyes thoughtful and questioning. Then slowly, deliberately, he reached for the TV with his right hand. I watched, thrilled and fascinated, as his right hand came down on the set like a crane with sticky gears and a drunken driver. His hand crash landed on the TV screen and slid off. Then he turned to me and grinned.

What should I do? Until now, we had always reacted with exaggerated delight whenever he attempted anything with his right hand. And Jonathan knew this. He wasn't daft. I turned away until I could keep my face straight, then I told him, as usual, that he was a clever boy using his right hand. "But," I added sternly, "you are still not allowed to switch the TV on."

It was Jonathan's persistence that was now enabling him, not only to sit up without falling over, but to stand. And then, supported under the arms, he took his first, very wobbly steps. His wobbly walk soon changed into what looked suspiciously like a miniature goosestep as his stiff little legs jerked alternately up and down, while Brian or I shuffled along behind, bent almost double as we held him upright.

And then, Brian and I had a meeting with Frau Trepp-Jung and a senior physiotherapist who was visiting the area. We proudly told her how Jonathan was starting to walk with support, and how, most days, we took him into the forest where he would insist on walking for quite long distances. The senior physio-therapist looked horrified and told us sternly that we could cause irreversible damage by encouraging Jonathan to walk too soon. We left the meeting feeling confused and upset, and for the rest of the week we were torn between wanting to help Jonathan walk, and fearing to push him too hard.

Then we reminded ourselves that we knew Jonathan better

than she did. In fact, she didn't know him at all. We knew when he was ready to learn a new skill, and he was ready to walk. He loved walking. So we carried on. It was reassuring to have Frau Trepp-Jung agree with us, but it was months before we could completely lose the fear that we might inadvertently be harming our son.

In the meantime, his balance was steadily improving. And by the time of my graduation in May, when Jonathan was twenty-one months, he was charging up and down the room with his push-along horse, screeching with laughter every time he rammed the sideboard at the end, rattling my best china inside. Like all toddlers, he didn't have a very good braking system. We had no doubts now that one day Jonathan would walk unaided.

Some weeks prior to my graduation, I had received a phone call from the University of Maryland's main European campus in Munich. The caller told me that I was the winner of the Colonel Bentley Award, one that is presented annually to the University's European Division graduate with the highest grade point average. That year, he informed me, there were just under a thousand graduates.

I could hardly believe it. And I thought about what my father had said about girls being too stupid to learn. I had proved him wrong — as Jonathan was proving the neurologist wrong. In a way, I wished that my dad could be there at the graduation. I wanted to show him that I wasn't stupid, that not only had I graduated Summa cum Laude with a degree in Psychology, but that I had also won a coveted award. But when I thought about it, I realised that the two people I most wanted there, besides Jonathan, were Brian and my friend, Pam. To my great delight, I discovered that the graduation coincided with half term, so she was able to come.

Over the years, Pam and I had discovered shared interests: travel, history, and Jane Austen. And during her annual visits we often sat over breakfast, discussing the finer points of the Austen novels, until we realised, with amazement, that it was time to get lunch. But not this day. Today was the first of two days of graduation festivities held at Heidelberg, about an hour's drive

111

away. And today we would be joining about 500 graduates, each with two guests, for a boat trip on the Neckar, a lazy river that meandered through the steep wooded hills of the Odenwald. It was a beautiful sunny day, and as I leaned on the deck of the boat, gazing up at the massive bulk of Heidelberg castle towering over the town and river, I felt that I had stepped into a fairytale. Then, as I looked at Jonathan, bouncing on his Auntie Pam's knee as she sat chatting to Brian, I thought how lucky I was to have two dreams come true.

The following day, having donned my cap and gown, I joined the procession of graduates waiting to enter the auditorium, where friends and relatives were already seated, the children having been settled in the crèche. We were placed in alphabetical order — except for me. As the winner of the Colonel Bentley Award, I was kept to the last. I thought wryly that perhaps being the odd one out wasn't such a bad thing after all.

The proceedings began: the welcome, greetings, then addresses by the two speakers, Hans-Dietrich Genscher, then Foreign Minister of the Federal Republic of Germany, and Vernon A. Walters, the US Ambassador to Germany. Then, the president of the University's main campus in Maryland conferred the degrees. When at last they got to me, I stood looking out over the sea of faces while the president gave a brief history of the award, saying that it had been inaugurated seven years previously, and that if I had graduated in any of the past seven years, I would still have won it.

I was amazed. The top graduate out of an estimated 7,000! I wondered how on earth I had done it, as I had been on autopilot for most of that last year. Sometimes I'd gone into exams feeling too tired to even pick up a pen, my brain dominated by one thought: that I wanted to go home and crawl into bed. But I had come through. And now I was so very glad that I had persevered to the end. And as the president handed me the silver trophy, and applause broke out in the auditorium, I was thinking that, on this occasion, the reality had exceeded the fantasy; never in my wildest dreams had I imagined this.

After the ceremony, there was a buffet tea in the marquee. I hardly had time to eat as graduates from countries throughout

Europe, from Britain in the west to Turkey in the east, asked me, "Aren't you the winner of the Colonel Bentley Award?"

Many asked me how I had done it, if I worked or if I was a full-time student. And when I told them that I counselled two days a week, and that I had a small son with cerebral palsy, the usual response was, "That is more than a full-time job!"

And looking proudly at Jonathan, stepping out across the grass and saying "Ga-ga," while his Auntie Pam, immaculate as usual in her favourite green, supported him from behind, I thought, yes it certainly is. And I couldn't decide which was the greater achievement, getting Jonathan on his feet or graduating with such high honours. All I knew was that I couldn't have done anything without God. And I had a sudden feeling that God was laughing, that he was enjoying this day as much as I was.

After the buffet, the four of us walked around the grounds. At one point I took off my cap and placed it on Jonathan's head. He chuckled, took it off, turned it around in his hand, then put it back on his head. There was no mirror this time to send him into fits of giggles. But, as if through a mirror, I dimly saw Brian's vision being fulfilled, and Jonathan receiving *his* degree while I, the proud mother, looked on.

My gaze came back to the present, to a scene that I was reluctant to leave, and that I wanted to hold in my mind forever: the grounds with the smell of trampled grass, green in the bright sunshine and dappled with flickering shadows from groves of trees, proudly displaying their fresh new leaves; the marquee with its red and white striped awnings; and the clusters of graduates in caps and gowns, their blackness a vivid contrast to the bright spring finery of their guests. I did several laps of honour before finally dragging myself away. Everyone has their moment of glory. And this was mine.

Two years from now, I hoped, it would be Brian's turn. Apart from a few weekend seminars, he had dropped out of university after Jonathan's birth so that I could finish my degree. Now that I had graduated, he was resuming his studies while I stayed home and babysat. And maybe, I thought, this time next year Jonathan will be doing *his* lap of honour.

When the neurologist had said that Jonathan might never walk, we had made up our minds that we would prove him wrong. But we had expected it to take five, maybe ten years. The way Jonathan was going, he would probably walk unaided sometime during his second year. The terrible twos! I hated that expression. I preferred to think of it as the terrific twos. I was convinced that this coming year would be terrific, an exciting year full of new beginnings. I had a gut feeling that it would be the year Jonathan took his first independent step and said his first recognisable word.

As I fastened Jonathan in his car seat, I smiled at him, my thoughts lost in a sunny afterglow. He smiled back at me as his eye caught mine — just one eye. The other was gazing at some spot over my right shoulder. A shadow seemed to fall across us. Yes, Jonathan would walk and talk. But what about seeing? How much could he see? The shadow went as quickly as it came. Today had been terrific. The next big event, in August, would be Jonathan's second birthday, and that would be terrific — the start of the terrific twos!

# Chapter 11

The terrific twos began with three firsts for Jonathan, one of which we could have done without. Two days before his second birthday, we had set off for our holiday destination, a fisherman's cottage on the coast of Brittany. It was a horrific journey. The temperature was 40°C, and we were stuck for hours in a traffic jam on the ring road around Paris, with no shade. The heat was unbearable, our clothes were wringing wet, we were sticking to the car seats, and there was nowhere to go. When the traffic began moving again we decided we'd had enough. We had now been on the road for nine hours. So we stopped at the next town, Chartres, and found a hotel for the night.

We had just unpacked a few essentials and were about to have a cooling shower and change of clothes when Jonathan was sick all over his travel cot. So we spent the next hour cleaning up. We then spent a restless night in a hot, smelly room, and set off again late the next morning, hoping that today would be cooler.

But again, it was an unbearable 40°C. And again, as soon as we arrived at our destination, Jonathan was sick. After another seven hours travelling, cooped up in a car while the sun blazed relentlessly from a cloudless sky, we were all in desperate need of a cool sea breeze and a general unwind. So when we'd cleaned Jonathan up again, had a drink and unloaded the car, we headed for the sea and a long, refreshing walk.

It was early evening when we arrived back at the cottage. It was still stifling hot inside, so we immediately opened all the windows and the front door. Then, while Brian fed Jonathan, I unpacked the cases. We settled Jonathan in his cot wearing only a nappy. Then, as it slowly grew dark, we sat in the large kitchen enjoying a leisurely meal and the cool night breeze, now wafting in from the courtyard outside.

Later, we checked on Jonathan, and as Brian shone his torch on the cot, we gasped in horror at the sight thrown up in its beam. The cot was crawling with dozens and dozens of black, ugly mosquitoes. Brian now flashed his torch around the room, and we could hardly believe what we saw. They were everywhere, swarms of them — on the walls, ceiling, curtains, furniture.... Never in our lives had we seen so many. We spent two hours swatting the things before we fell, exhausted, into bed.

The next morning, Jonathan's birthday, we were shocked and appalled to discover that he was covered from head to foot in bites. The red lumps poked through his hair and dotted his face; they rose up in long, scarlet lines on his arms and legs; they ran together in red, suffused clumps on his chest and back; they swelled up between his fingers and toes. We stared at him, open-mouthed, while Jonathan grinned back, seemingly not at all affected by the bites, although no part of his little body had been spared — except the part covered by his nappy.

Brian was all for going straight home, but I thought there must be a way around the problem. I looked around the room, wondering what we could use as a mosquito net, and then I saw the net curtain hanging over the glass door. It would fit his cot perfectly. And although it was Sunday, I thought there must be a chemist open somewhere, and we could stock up with repellents and soothing creams. And if we shut the windows and door before it got dark, we would hopefully not be invaded again to quite the same extent.

While I was working out how to prevent the same thing happening again, Brian was counting Jonathan's bites. There were 47 of them. What a way to start his birthday! But, possibly because they were his first mosquito bites, Jonathan suffered no ill effects, not even a vague itch. And this, more than anything, decided us to stay for the entire fortnight as planned.

Jonathan looked very spectacular as, cooing and chuckling as usual, he opened his birthday presents. Then, after breakfast, spent avoiding Jonathan's toy plane that he kept zooming across the table, we set off for the beach. And there, he experienced another first: his first paddle in the sea.

He could now walk with only a hand to hold onto, and he set off with his daddy, giggling as the sand moved beneath his bare feet, throwing him off balance. He walked confidently into the sea, seemingly undaunted by its vastness. And from where I sat, minding his clothes and towels, and brand new bucket and spade, I could hear his chuckles, clear and distinct above the babble of voices around me, as Brian picked him up and swung him backwards and forwards through the gentle waves.

Later that day was another first: his first ice lolly. His daddy held it for him while Jonathan eagerly took a bite. Immediately he recoiled, his face a picture of shock and amazement. Then, slowly he grinned, and opened his mouth for more. And he sucked and slurped and giggled while an ever-widening circle of orange spread around his mouth, and the sticky juice ran down his bare chest between the mosquito bites, and over Brian's hand and down his arm, dripping from his elbow onto the hot sand, making pitted, squiggly patterns on its flattened surface.

Jonathan took in everything during that holiday. Everything, be it a lighthouse on a rocky outcrop, a bustling, narrow street, or the standing stones at Carnac, was a thing of beauty and wonder. He was especially fascinated by the light from stained glass windows in the many baroque churches we visited. Sitting in his stroller, he would clap his hands and laugh as his eyes followed the luminous streams of blue, red and gold that swirled around sturdy pillars, rippled over the pews, and spread like liquid fire across the marble floors. It was at times like this that we believed there was nothing wrong with Jonathan's eyes.

The holiday ended too soon. And so did our belief that Jonathan could see normally. We had resumed the "What-can-you-see-with-your-left-eye?" games, and although Jonathan didn't mind having his left eye covered, he continued to become distraught if we tried covering his right. We decided to go back to the paediatrician and ask if he could recommend another ophthalmist. We wanted a second opinion. Dr Lieb suggested Herr Professor Ungeduld, an eminent children's eye specialist in Frankfurt. He was one of the best in Germany.

The Herr Professor held his practice at the University Hospital, and right from the first moment we hated the place. The eye-clinic building was old and decrepit, and a narrow corridor at the top of a steep flight of stairs served as a waiting room. There were no windows, and nothing to look at except the people sitting opposite, and doctors and patients coming in and out of the doors at either end. And unlike the other surgeries we frequented, there was nothing for children to play with.

The specialist was an old man, and although we had no cause to doubt his reputation, we never quite felt that we trusted him. And we certainly didn't like the way he handled Jonathan. He expected a little two-year-old to cooperate: to look in the direction ordered, to stare at a light without blinking, to keep still. And when Jonathan didn't immediately obey, he became snappy and impatient. Jonathan underwent several tests, then the Herr Professor told us that the optic nerve of Jonathan's left eye was severely atrophied from lack of use. He said that Jonathan had probably never used that eye, and he prescribed glasses and eye patches. Jonathan had to wear a patch over his right eye for eight hours per day, two days out of every three, to encourage him to use the lazy eye.

Although we didn't particularly like the Herr Professor, we were grateful that he had recognised something was wrong, and was giving Jonathan some treatment. Also, we now had an explanation for his inconsistent reactions to moving objects when he was a baby, as he couldn't then turn his head to the right.

Just as, from the first moment, we had hated the eye clinic, so from the first moment Jonathan hated his glasses and patch. He kept taking his glasses off and throwing them away. And as for his patch! That was a nightmare. He screamed and kicked and squirmed whenever I tried fixing it in place, then clawed at it until it came unstuck at the edges and he could cheat by peering around it. I frequently spent the entire day sticking it back again. And on warm days, when Jonathan's face became sweaty and the patch came unstuck by itself, I often felt close to despair.

Nothing helped. We tried playing at pirates, but Jonathan didn't want to be a pirate. We tried, much against our inclination, bribing him with treats, but Jonathan wasn't interested in sweets, or offers of cake and juice when we went out shopping. We tried jollity, persuasion, explanation, commands.... But to no avail. Jonathan flatly refused to wear either the glasses or the patch.

118

At the next check-up we told the Herr Professor about our difficulties, and he said that the patch was the more important of the two, and not to worry too much about the glasses. So when we got home, we made a big deal of telling Jonathan that he didn't need to wear his glasses any more, in the hope that it would stop the daily Battle of the Eye Patch. But no such luck. The battle intensified as he now screamed louder, squirmed more, and violently swung his head from side to side as I tried sticking the patch firmly in place. But the worst part was seeing our happy, curious, outgoing child turn into a pathetic little scrap who whined constantly, cried at the smallest thing, and took not the slightest notice of anything around him. It was heartbreaking.

We were thankful that Jonathan had only to wear the patch on two days out of three, because on the third day he became himself again: laughing, chuckling, and poking his nose into everything, whether it had been forbidden him or not. We often wondered if we were doing the right thing, or if we should abandon the treatment. But we had to think of the future. We kept telling ourselves that all this hassle would be worth it in the end, and that Jonathan would be grateful we had persevered.

It was now late October, a no-patch day, and Jonathan was poking his nose into everything, getting in the way, as once again I was packing, not this time for a holiday, but for a university course. Brian was studying art history as his minor subject, and since it was an interest we shared, we had done several courses together; in my case as electives. We had studied Dutch painting in Amsterdam, Impressionism in Paris, German Expressionism in Cologne, and Modern Art in London. And Brian was preparing now to study Contemporary Art at the Louisiana Art Gallery, near Elsinore in Denmark.

Although I was no longer a student, Jane, the tutor, was happy for me and Jonathan to go along too, and even for me to attend tours and lectures when Jonathan had his long afternoon nap. Brian and I had decided to give him a break from his eye patch, and we were hopeful that, without this stress, he would walk more than the two or three steps he was now managing alone, as he staggered from one of us to the other.

Denmark was much colder than Germany. But every day the sun shone, the sky was a clear, dazzling blue, and the trees a glorious profusion of reds, orange and gold. So every day, as well as looking at the paintings and sculptures in the Louisiana, or sitting in the cafe looking out on green lawns and the cold blue-grey of the Baltic Sea, Jonathan and I spent a lot of time playing in the grounds. And it was there, on those green lawns, among Henry Moore, Giacometti and Calder sculptures, that Jonathan took his first independent steps.

It happened that the three of us were together, and we had our video camera with us, so we were able to film him as, half-way between Brian and me, he suddenly changed direction and went toddling off, away from us, across the lush grass. From the back he looked like Charlie Chaplin, his little flat feet turned outwards as he moved jerkily along, his lower right arm bent stiffly away from his body and needing only a twirling walking stick to make the picture complete.

There was a path bisecting the lawn, and as Jonathan approached it I grew anxious in case he fell over on the hard gravel. But just before he reached the path he did a very unsteady U-turn and, beaming from ear to ear, walked back to me and fell laughing into my outstretched arms. And now we were all laughing. We laughed and hugged and laughed some more. We were delirious with joy. Jonathan had proved the neurologist wrong! He could walk! And far, far sooner than we had ever imagined. He was two years and three months.

Immediately we went to find Jane, to tell her the good news, and soon the whole class knew — and anyone else who cared to listen. And as Jonathan did a little lap of honour, proudly showing off his new skill, everyone was laughing. All who hear will laugh with me, I thought, and my heart was so light that I felt in danger of taking off. It was wonderful! God was wonderful! And tomorrow, we were going to see wonderful Copenhagen. It seemed that life had nothing more to offer.

We came back to earth gradually, with the ending of the course and the return to our normal routine. But even with our feet back on the ground, we never quite lost the wonder of it, and as day followed day and Jonathan walked more steadily and fell less frequently, we felt so very, very thankful. And then, one day, he pointed to a banana and said very clearly and distinctly, "Nana."

Such a little word! But what a wealth of meaning for Brian and me. Ever since that car ride to the Black Forest over a year ago when, for the first time, he had started to babble, we had believed that one day Jonathan would talk. But with Broca's area of the brain affected, there had always been that nagging fear: the thought, but what if? That one little word banished the fear for ever. It had gone, never to return. We knew now that Jonathan would be able to talk. And we were over the moon.

His next word was "Dadda," and then "Mamma." Then came "Jaja," his name for himself. And then, "yes." We were astonished. We had always thought that one of the first things a child said was "no." But then, we rarely said no to Jonathan. Usually we were telling him, "Yes, go ahead. You can do it."

Soon he had a vocabulary of a few dozen words. Then he began putting words together. His first phrase was, "Open door."

This too wasn't surprising, considering the number of times — so many times, every day, three hundred and sixty-five days a year, for two long years — that we had reminded him to open his fingers. And we thought how very symbolic this was as we now took him through an open door into a new world: the world of shared speech.

Right from his birth, we had always talked to Jonathan about anything and everything, and we had enthusiastically read nursery rhymes and poetry and stories to him. But now, more than ever, we filled his life with words. And Jonathan hung onto every word, his eyes wide and eager, following the movement of our lips or scanning the lines of a book, his mouth moving silently, every now and then attempting to say something out loud. He especially loved a book of tongue twisters a friend had recently bought him, and he creased up with laughter every time I stumbled over a word or mixed up the vowels or consonants. Words were fun!

But after this little spurt, he slowed down, probably because the constant battles with the eye patch were wearing him

121

out, and because, on those two days out of three, he couldn't see properly. Also, walking still required a lot of concentration and effort as he couldn't bend his right ankle sufficiently to put his foot flat on the floor. The muscles of his right leg were wasted, and this leg was now about half an inch shorter than the other. There was talk of surgery, splints, and a built-up shoe. But the orthopaedic surgeon felt that, at this stage, while Jonathan was able to put some weight on his right leg to stimulate growth, we should wait. And we were happy to wait. Jonathan had enough to contend with.

Christmas had now come and gone, and so had another New Year. We had spent the festive season at home, in Germany, as we had two years earlier when Jonathan was a baby. Then we had stood on the balcony watching the fireworks, and I had resolved that one day Jonathan would stand there with us, bringing in the New Year. This had now become a possibility, although at only two, Jonathan had been tucked up in his cot at midnight, fast asleep. And the uppermost thought in our minds as we ushered in 1991 had been Jonathan's British citizenship.

It had now been over a year since we applied, and we had heard nothing. And we were getting anxious, wondering if we had given a good enough reason for it to be granted. We had really struggled with the question, "Why do you want to apply for British citizenship?"

We had thought of all sorts of reasons. We had debated saying what a hassle it was getting a transit visa for Jonathan every time we drove through France to England. We had considered saying how difficult it would be later on having a son going through a different customs area to ourselves. And although we had giggled at Jonathan's visitor's permit to England, stating that he could stay for six months as long as he didn't work, we anticipated that this would be a major problem if we moved back to England when he was in his teens. But in the end we simply wrote, "Naturally, we want our son to be the same nationality as ourselves."

January and February passed. The snow came and went.

And finally, on March 6th, we received the long-awaited reply. British citizenship had been granted, and we could now apply for a British passport. The relief was tremendous.

Jonathan now had three nationalities: American, German, and British. But at age eighteen he would have to drop one of them. What a decision to have to make! We hoped that he would make the right one. But, his having cerebral palsy did at least mean that he wouldn't have to be too concerned about military service in his countries of choice, in Germany compulsory for two years, and in America should there be another Korean or Vietnam war.

In the meantime, Jonathan was continuing to fight his own little battles — in addition to the Battle of the Eye Patch. We had long realised that he was a fighter, and that he didn't give up easily. And he had achieved so very much in such a short space of time. Jonathan was very proud of his achievements, and his most often repeated sentence, said with a look of triumph or determination, depending on whether it was something he had done or was about to do, was, "Jaja do it."

This was partly a typical two-year-old's belief in his own omnipotence, and teaching a child that he can't do everything without making him feel inadequate is difficult. And a constant drain on one's patience. But when that child is handicapped, it is especially so. We wanted Jonathan to do things for himself, but we also wanted him to learn when and how to ask for help, and how to accept that help gracefully. He began to learn this fine balance, I think, the day he tried to push his stroller up the steep hill near our home that led to the Taunus forest.

Jonathan was "helping" me push the stroller, as he often did, using his one good hand, when suddenly he pushed me away, saying, "Jaja do it."

I told him that the hill was too steep and the stroller too heavy, but he wouldn't listen. "Jaja do it," he said stubbornly.

So I took my hands away, merely keeping my foot against the rear wheel to stop the stroller rolling backwards. Jonathan pushed and shoved and strained, saying over and over, "Jaja do it." But the stroller wouldn't budge.

He was getting angry, so surreptitiously I tried to help him. But unfortunately, he noticed, and he now began throwing a full-scale tantrum, pushing me harder than ever and screaming, "JAJA DO IT! JAJA DO IT!"

At that point I decided that he would just have to learn for himself that he couldn't do it, and I prayed that no one was watching as I stood there, pretending he wasn't with me, while the poor little mite repeatedly flung his weight against the stroller to make it roll uphill. It seemed an awful long time before he gave up and said, "Mummy help."

I helped him only too willingly, and with a great sense of relief. And when he had calmed down I explained that, although I was glad that he had tried, there are some things that we cannot do alone. He seemingly got the message. And so, I think, did I, as I remembered the many times I had pushed friends away, saying dismissively, "I can manage, thank you."

And how many times, I wondered, had I pushed God away, and then wondered why he wasn't there when things got tough?

As we approached the end of the terrific twos, we felt that we were coming to the end of a long, uphill struggle. Against all odds, Jonathan was overcoming his handicap. We had taught him to roll over, crawl, sit up, climb onto a chair, and finally to walk. He was trying to use his right hand, and he was starting to talk. The twos really had been terrific!

The only disappointment had been his left eye: at each check-up we had been told that, in spite of the eye patch treatment, there was no improvement. But that would change next year, we told ourselves. And life generally would be on a more even keel. Next year would be a year of consolidation. Jonathan's sight would improve, he would walk more easily, and he would talk more fluently. It would be the year of the open door. We could hardly wait to go through that door, and explore the other side.

# Chapter 12

As we entered with Jonathan the new and exciting world of speech, the first thing we discovered was that, far from being on an even keel, life was bumpier than ever. The more Jonathan talked, the more we found new problems to contend with — and new frustrations. The main problem was a phenomenon that sometimes occurs with cerebral palsy, known as "cocktail conversation". This became increasingly evident as Jonathan reached his third birthday.

We were filming him as he opened his presents in our holiday apartment in Holland, revelling in his clear, musical baby voice, and smiling at his comments. We had bought him, among other things, a Fireman Sam book.

"Fiemasam," he told me.

"Yes, that's Fireman Sam," I agreed.

"Fiemasam," he repeated.

I agreed again.

"Fiemasam," said Jonathan.

"Yes," I replied wearily.

"Fiemasam."

He would repeat the same thing over and over, sometimes up to twenty times. It was as if his brain had got stuck and was going round and round in the same groove. Ignoring him made no difference. He had to play out his one word or phrase until, for some unknown reason, his brain suddenly switched on to something else. It drove us demented.

Jonathan also tended to ask the same question over and over, with slight variations. A typical example occurred on a visit to Dr Lieb's. We told Jonathan that he could play with a toy garage in the corner while we talked. "This garage?" he asked, as he immediately began rolling a car down its ramp.

"Yes," we told him.

"On the floor?"

"Yes, the garage on the floor."

"Play with it?"

"Yes, you can play with it."

"On the floor."

"Yes, the garage on the floor."

"Play with garage."

"Yes, you can play with the garage."

When he was a baby, we used to look at his right arm, which at that stage didn't look deformed, and we used to want to grab it, to make it do something. It just didn't seem right that it should hang there, so useless. And now, as he chatted away like any normal child, we tended to forget that his endless repetitions arose, in part, from his condition, and we often wanted to say to him, "For goodness sake, shut up and get on with it!"

The months passed, and as Jonathan began speaking more fluently, we made yet another discovery: that our son was a little chatterbox. He never stopped, from the moment he woke up till the moment he fell asleep. And after three years of worry, wondering if he would ever talk, I now sometimes wished that he'd shut up and give my reeling brain a few minutes respite. And yet, this open door into the world of speech had also brought us into a world of fun and laughter. We laughed a lot during this period, thinking with amusement that no one reaps what they sow more than parents of a three year old. We were now having all our own sayings played back to us, complete with exact imitation of our tone of voice, gestures, and facial expressions.

How glad we were that we had focused so much on the positive, that we had constantly encouraged Jonathan, and that we had never put him down. It was so nice, if somewhat ludicrous, to hear a little tot saying very earnestly when I danced around the room with him, "You did that very nicely, Mummy." Or, when I'd eaten up all my dinner, "Well done. Mummy." Or, if I dropped something, "Never mind. Mummy. Try again."

Often, Jonathan's habit of repeating everything exactly as he heard it kept us chuckling for an entire evening, like the time we were having family prayers. Jonathan was repeating a little prayer after me, and in the middle of it I happened to burp. Jonathan faithfully repeated word for word what I had just said — complete with burp.

It wasn't only us that Jonathan imitated, but the people on his cassettes. We had bought him a cassette recorder the previous Christmas, with knobs for him to press, adding drumbeats, cymbal clashes and animal sounds to whatever he was playing. The cassette recorder soon proved to be a God-send, giving me welcome breaks from his non-stop chatter, and it wasn't long before Jonathan knew every poem and song by heart, and could repeat every story, with all the variations of tone and emphasis.

As well as interjecting a quick burst of drums or cymbals, or a lion's roar or dog's bark, usually at a most inappropriate moment, Jonathan often stopped the tape while he came to ask me the meaning of a word he didn't understand. So he soon developed a very wide vocabulary, and his use of long words was another source of amusement. He loved the sounds of words like "ingenuity" or "magnificent", and he would repeat them over and over, trying them out in different sentences, whether they belonged there or not.

And then there were the occasions when he didn't have the word for what he wanted to say, like the time when his hands went crinkly after staying too long in the bath. He wanted to know why they had gone gravelly. Or the time when, having explained that I was putting cream on my face to make it nice and soft, he asked, "If you don't put cream on your face, will it go crunchy?"

There were also those times when he misunderstood or misheard a word. During one cold spell I frequently asked him to shut the living room door because there was a draught coming through. Normally, Jonathan never obeyed without question, and he usually had to put up at least a token resistance. But this particular request he always obeyed with alacrity, and I always wondered why. Then one day, after I had asked him as usual to shut the door because there was a draught coming through, he raced to my side and stood very close to me, his frightened eyes fixed on the open door.

"Why didn't you shut the door?" I asked him.

He edged closer and, with his eyes still fixed on the door, said with a touch of bravado, "Jaja leave it open. Jaja want to see giraffe coming through."

We never knew whether he was relieved or disappointed that his giraffe was nothing more than a gust of air, although for a long time after that our house was full of pretend giraffes who trooped through that door one after the other, all day long. And giraffes were a never-ending topic of conversation.

Yes, Jonathan was certainly talking more. And he was walking more steadily and for longer distances. And wonder of wonders! He could run! His gait was stiff and jerky, but that didn't matter. Like any normal child, he was having fun. One of his favourite pastimes was chasing pigeons, something he did every time we went shopping in Wiesbaden. With a whoop and a yell he would dash off, darting in and out of the shoppers, while I tried to keep up with the stroller and the poor bewildered pigeon toddled off, just out of his arm's reach. Only when Jonathan's flailing left arm and excited laughs became a bit too much would the pigeon give a disdainful toss of its head and fly up into the nearest tree.

Over a two year period we filmed Jonathan chasing pigeons, not only in Wiesbaden, but in the Town Hall Square in Bonn, in Trafalgar Square in London, in the park in The Hague, in Mozartplatz in Salzburg, in the English Gardens in Munich, in the shopping square at Arles, and on the green in Sête, a seaside town in Languedoc. There he varied things by also chasing a French girl.

Not only could Jonathan run, he could also pick up a ball with two hands; although he used the back, rather than the palm, of his right hand. And, he could kick a ball. At first he kept losing his balance and landing with a bump on his bottom as he swung his left leg at the ball. But with practice he was able to stand for a second or two on his wasted right leg, and remain upright even while he kicked. Soon he developed a very powerful kick, giving Brian and me plenty of exercise retrieving the ball.

It was at this time that he asked me, "Mummy, if I kick my ball very hard, will it go through the clouds?"

"Yes," I told him.

"If it goes through the clouds, will it land in heaven?"

128

I said that it would, thinking that, at three and a half, he was not yet ready for a theological discussion on the location of heaven.

"If it lands in heaven, will Jesus kick it back to me?"

"Yes, I'm sure he will," I replied promptly, and with absolute assurance.

Jonathan nodded, and went away smiling, while I sat pondering his question. Suddenly, a picture flashed into my mind of God seated on the throne, with Jesus at his right hand, and the four and twenty elders bowing down and worshipping, and a big red and yellow ball bouncing into their midst. And I started to giggle. And I giggled and giggled and giggled. When Jonathan eventually returned, I was holding onto my aching ribs and tears of laughter were running down my face. He gave me an amazed look and asked me what I was laughing at.

"I was thinking about Jesus kicking your ball back," I squeaked. And Jonathan started giggling too. I don't know what he was picturing, but it was a long time before either of us could talk coherently again.

After this, I often imagined Jesus joining in our ball games and enjoying the fun, as I expect he did with the children of Palestine during the short time he spent on this little planet of ours.

Jonathan now had more freedom of movement as he was no longer wearing bulky nappies, and it was lovely watching him running about in his new, slimline shorts. We had only recently potty trained him, and it had been a cinch; so different to how it had been with our foster child. When Mark came to us at two, we had been horrified to discover that no one in the children's home had even attempted to potty train him. And, possibly because we were trying to impress the social workers, we began immediately, long before he was ready. We had an awful time of it. And a year later he was still having accidents.

With Jonathan we waited until we knew the time was right, and in only three weeks he was dry. And he never had an accident. Bowel training took a little longer. It wasn't that he did it in his pants, or on the floor, or anywhere else. He simply refused to do it at all. Instead he would do what appeared to be some kind of war dance, yelling and stomping while refusing to sit on his potty or the toilet, and insisting that he didn't need to go. I was very patient with him for a few weeks. Then one day I sat him firmly on the loo and told him crossly to stop messing around and get on with it. And he did. And from that day he never looked back.

Not only was Jonathan out of nappies, he no longer needed to wear bibs, as the constant dribbling had stopped. He was fast changing from a cute little toddler into a lovely little boy. And he was noticeably becoming more independent as he walked and ran, and played and chattered from morning till night about anything and everything, only occasionally lying on the floor and doing absolutely nothing, except perhaps daydreaming. But — and there was a big but — this was only on one day out of three. On the other days, he tore constantly at his eye patch, moped, whined, and threw tantrums.

Jonathan had now been wearing his patch for eighteen months, but his left eye was not getting any better. And then, the Professor told us that there was no point continuing the treatment as he had only 2% vision in that eye. We were devastated, and horrified to think that for eighteen months, two days out of three, we had been shutting Jonathan away in a world of darkness. And shutting him away when we had wanted so much for him to see and experience all the beauty and wonder of the world around him.

At first we couldn't accept it, so we got a second, and then a third opinion. And only then, when everyone confirmed that Jonathan was technically blind in one eye, did we face up to the awful truth. But at least the Battle of the Eye Patch was over. And, apart from having to think about surgery at some future date to correct his squint, we could now forget about his eyes and concentrate on other things. We also had the consolation of a thought expressed by one of the workers at the Child Development Center, where Jonathan was still spending two days a week while I worked as a counsellor. "Jonathan sees more with one eye," she told me, "than most children do with two."

It was ironic that a favourite verse at this time was "Two little eyes":

Two little eyes to look to God;
Two little ears to hear his Word;
Two little feet to walk in his ways;
Two little lips to sing his praise;
Two little hands to do his will;
And one little heart to love him still.

It was while reciting this one evening that Jonathan suddenly got down from his chair, did a circuit of the living room, and sat down again. "Why did you do that?" I asked.

He gave me a questioning look, as if wondering why I was asking the obvious, and explained patiently, "I was walking in his ways."

At times Jonathan seemed to think his mother a complete idiot, like the time he noticed a photograph of Brian and me, taken long before he was born. He wanted to know where Jaja was, and I explained that he hadn't been born yet, reminding him of a video we had recently watched about a little colt being born and growing up into a beautiful young horse. Jonathan pondered this, obviously dissatisfied with my answer. Then he said firmly, "No," while his frown deepened.

He continued deep in thought. Then, suddenly, his face lit up. He'd clearly had an idea. He gave a little affirmative nod, threw me a pitying glance, and with all the authority of a three year old informed me, "Jaja took the photo."

We had thought that young children accepted everything without question — except for the "Why?" question — but not Jonathan. When I told him one day that the earth on which we lived was like an enormous ball spinning in the sky, he gave me a look of withering contempt, as if to say, who do you think you're kidding! Then he shook his head and said very emphatically, "No."

Jonathan had entered the "Why?" stage — and the "What-would-happen-if?" stage — with a vengeance. And since he wanted to know the whys and wherefores of everything, telling him a story seemed to take forever. He would keep interrupting, wanting to know why there was a serpent in the Garden of Eden, why it could talk, why Moses cried when the princess opened the basket, what would have happened if he hadn't, why Jesus died on a cross, why he went back to heaven, why we can't see him.... His questions were endless. And they were not confined to stories. I couldn't even make a simple comment, like pointing out some cows in a field, without it leading to a long, tiring, and often circular discussion:

"Why are the cows lying down?" he would ask.

"I don't know," I would reply. "Perhaps they're tired."

"Why are they tired?"

"I expect they've been busy looking for nice grass to eat."

"Why do they eat grass?"

"Because grass tastes nice for cows."

"Why does grass taste nice for cows?"

"Because that's how God made them. He gave them special tummies for the grass to go into, and the grass makes them nice and strong."

"What would happen if it didn't?"

"Then they would feel weak and tired."

"What would happen if they felt weak and tired?"

At that point I usually gave up, my head spinning, as I wondered what on earth I'd got myself into. And yet, Brian and I were delighted with his avid curiosity, and we tried, as much as possible, to answer his many questions. We wanted him to stay curious, to retain his sense of wonder — as we had.


It was possibly because we had such enquiring minds, such an insatiable desire to find out about everything, that we both did so well at university. Brian had now graduated. And, he had just been informed that he was the winner of the Colonel Bentley Award for this graduation year, 1992. Since they had never before had two winners in the same family, they wanted to really go to town about it. And they asked us to arrive early so that we could both be photographed with the speakers: Manfred Rommel, the Mayor of Stuttgart and son of the famous Field

Marshal, and the rector of Irkutsk State University in Russia.

Pam came to Brian's graduation as she had to mine. And again, the weather was glorious; and the trees, newly clothed in their spring finery, spread their welcome shade for the graduates and their guests, gathered from all over Europe. It was like history repeating itself, but with a reversal: last time I had been the graduate and Brian a guest; this time he was the graduate and I was a guest. The other big difference was Jonathan. At my graduation he had sat on his Auntie Pam's knee during the boat trip and said, "Gaga."

Now, he sat at her side, chatting away about his clever daddy, and solemnly informing her that Mummy wasn't very good at maths, but Daddy had helped her with that, and then Daddy had made ever such a silly mistake in the exam and Mummy had beaten him. But Mummy used to be a nurse and she knows how to make Jaja's leg better when he falls over and hurts himself.

On the day of the graduation, the four of us were welcomed by university officials. Then Brian and I were photographed for an American newspaper, not only with Manfred Rommel and the Russian rector, but with William Schaefer, the Governor of the State of Maryland, and with the President of the University.

Later, when the procession of graduates entered the auditorium of the University Campus in Heidelberg, Brian was kept to the last, as I had been. Then, he was presented with his award. The president gave a speech, causing ripples of laughter as he speculated on which of us actually had the highest marks, and whether we argued about it. For various reasons, he explained, each of us could claim to be the better, although we had both achieved a perfect grade point average, having gained an "A" for every course.

Afterwards came the buffet tea, and the four of us were asked to join the university officials, speakers, and special guests in the VIP marquee. We felt very honoured, although in some ways we would have preferred to be with the other graduates. I was glad of the honour for Brian's sake. This, more than

133

anything, made *his* day extra special. And as we headed back home to Wehen, tired but happy after a long, eventful day, I thought, what a story we have to tell the grandchildren!

For the first time I was allowing myself to dream about a future for Jonathan: perhaps university, a fulfilling job, a loving wife and children; all the normal things that mothers of normal children dream about. And since Jonathan loved stories, and had developed an insatiable demand for them, I decided that the time had come to begin writing *his* story: to give him something special that he could treasure, and pass onto his children.

We had often told Jonathan the story of his birth and adoption; how we had prayed for a child, how he had grown in another lady's tummy, how she had prayed for someone to love and care for him because she wasn't very good with babies, and how God had brought him to us. Jonathan never tired of hearing this story. And he loved hearing how I had dressed him at the hospital in traditional German baby clothes — a white cotton jersey with matching cotton dungarees that had a blue fish embroidered on the front — and how I hadn't been able to fasten the buttons on the shoulder because, although it was the smallest size, it was too big for him.

His own story was possibly his favourite, although he seemed to equally enjoy stories of all kinds: Bible stories, fairy tales, classics such as Beatrix Potter's *Peter Rabbit* and *Jemima Puddleduck*, current favourites like Postman Pat and Thomas the Tank Engine, and made-up-as-you-go stories. And there were two occasions in particular when storytelling became the accepted routine. One was when I did my weekly ironing.

Ironing had always been my most hated chore, and before Jonathan was born I used to make it easier by playing background music. Now I had to tell one story after another while, with aching back, I worked my way through ever-increasing piles of clothes.

I had developed the habit of ironing in our bedroom so that, while I worked, Jonathan could play on our bed, out of harm's way. He loved bouncing on the bed, and eventually the ironing stories developed two main themes. In the earth-bound theme, Jonathan bounced so high that he flew right over the balcony and landed on the grass beneath, where he had tea with a family of rabbits. In the cloud theme, Jonathan bounced right up into the sky and landed on a cloud; sometimes on Nicky Nimbus, the rain cloud, but more often on Colin Cumulus, the pretty, white sunshine cloud.

At some point in the story, I usually joined him. So, while I worked away at my mundane task, Jonathan and I floated across the sky, having some fascinating conversations with Colin Cumulus and visiting all sorts of interesting countries. Sometimes we even managed to find the secret door into the cloud, and we'd find ourselves in a pink and white fairyland. And then, the ironing done, we would slide back to earth down the rainbow.

The other occasion when Jonathan demanded non-stop stories was when we went out in the car. As soon as Brian turned the ignition key, it switched Jonathan on as well. Like a tape with a pre-recorded message he would ask, "Will you tell me a story?"

When returning from a shopping trip, we always made him wait until we were out of the town. And once he had realised that he wouldn't get a story in a built-up area, he would also ask repeatedly, "Are we out of the town yet?"

Later still, as we tried teaching him to wait patiently, he would ask over and over, "Am I being patient? Am I being patient?"

I don't know about Jonathan, but we were learning patience. We had thought it hard having to repeat movements, and then instructions, over and over. But having to answer his non-stop questions and respond to his constant repetitions was more draining than I had ever imagined. And although I enjoyed having Jonathan at home, for the first time I began to look forward to him going to school. But this gave rise to a headache of a different kind.

When the adoption was finalised, we had put Jonathan's name down at our local kindergarten. And then we had been informed that we should have registered him at birth, because

135

there was such a long waiting list. Jonathan was now almost four, the age German children start kindergarten. And, as we had been forewarned, there were no vacancies. And neither were there likely to be any for a long time. In Germany, children don't start school until they are six or seven. As Jonathan's birthday is in August, he would be seven — another three years. It was a long time to wait.

Another problem was that, although we loved Germany, we weren't too happy with the German school system. Even if we got Jonathan into a mainstream school, he would likely be left behind as Germans tend to educate for conformity. We feared that his special needs would be neglected and his unique abilities and strengths ignored.

And then there was the problem of the language. We had planned bringing him up to be bilingual, but when he was diagnosed as having cerebral palsy, we decided to stick to one language: English. Of course, Jonathan heard German all the time, but he didn't seem to understand very much; and apart from a few words, he didn't speak it.

So, for the first time in fifteen years, we considered leaving Germany. But we didn't want to return to England. England was where I had been abused and rejected. It was where I had been prevented from going to university. It was where I'd had to give up my profession because I couldn't bear the pain of my childlessness. And it was where a much-loved foster child had been taken from us.

For a long time now, we had thought that we'd like to live in the United States. We had once spent a long holiday there, in four different states, and we had loved every minute of it. We had many friends there. We both had American degrees. And, although Jonathan was now a British citizen, America was his country of origin. Was America the answer?

# Chapter 13

We had expected, since Jonathan was American, that we would have no problems getting into the US. But this was not the case. As Jonathan was a minor, we could not move to the States on the basis of his nationality until he was eighteen. In order to get a resident's visa, Brian would first have to obtain work there. But no one would give him a job until he had a resident's visa. It was a Catch 22 situation. We tried everything, even writing to contacts we had made at Brian's graduation, including the Governor of Maryland. He was very helpful, sending Brian the addresses of several firms in that state, but to no avail. The only alternative was moving back to England. But we didn't want to even consider that. So we just let things drift.

In the meantime, we were going backwards and forwards to the orthopaedic workshop with Jonathan. He had been prescribed a night splint to stretch his right leg while he slept, and straighten his twisted foot, We didn't have the hassle with the night splint that we'd had with the eye patch. But, because we couldn't fully extend Jonathan's leg, we couldn't get the splint to fit comfortably, and it rubbed sores on his ankles and knees. In the end, they made one with a hinge so that, at first, Jonathan could have his knee slightly bent; and we straightened it, little by little, over time. His leg did catch up its growth a little, although it remained thin and wasted; such a contrast to his sturdy left leg. And although his foot became straighter, his tight Achilles tendon still prevented him from putting it flat on the floor. He walked with that foot on tiptoe.

We were also going backwards and forwards to the dentist. In spite of a healthy, well-balanced diet, Jonathan's back molars went bad almost as soon as they came through. The dentist thought this was possibly the result of calcium deficiency in pregnancy, and he assured us that his second teeth would be stronger and healthier. He prescribed fluoride tablets, which slowed down the rot, but didn't stop it completely. So the day came when, at four and a half, Jonathan had to have fillings.

We explained to Jonathan what the dentist would do, telling him honestly but also, we hoped, reassuringly, that it might hurt a bit. But I don't think we prepared him sufficiently for the noise of the drill. It terrified him, and he started to scream. The dentist stopped immediately and, having calmed Jonathan down and given him some of his instruments to play with, said that it would be best if he had the fillings done under general anaesthetic. Like us, he didn't want Jonathan to be permanently afraid of dentists. He arranged an appointment at the hospital, and although this was for only a few weeks later, by this time it was decided to remove three of his molars and fill the fourth.

At the hospital they gave Jonathan his pre-med in the waiting room, so that he could continue playing, and after a few minutes he went completely floppy. He lay on the floor like a rag doll, giggling at his own helplessness; and he was still giggling when the anaesthetist, with a broad grin, picked him up and carried him over his shoulder to the operating theatre.

I had been anxious before we even got to the hospital. But now I could hardly sit still, and I became increasingly tense as I imagined allergic reactions, cardiac arrest, and goodness knows what. After ten minutes or so, I could sit still no longer, and I leapt up and went to get some coffee. On the way to the hospital restaurant I passed the operating theatre, and I was amazed to discover that all one side of it was glass, so anyone could look in. I couldn't see Jonathan, but I could see the surgeons bending over him. They were talking and smiling, and I breathed a sigh of relief. So far, everything was okay.

After it was all over, I sat with Jonathan in the recovery room, while Brian went back to work. I felt so frustrated and helpless as I looked at his poor little swollen face and the blood oozing from the corner of his mouth. I would have given any-thing to be able to swap places with him. He shouldn't have had to go through that.

The minutes and the hours passed, and I continued to sit there. I had told Jonathan that I would be there when he woke up, and I intended to be there, however long it took. I remembered my dad visiting me in hospital when I was four, after I'd had my appendix out. I remembered how amazed I'd been that dad should come to see *me*. I had gazed at him, wonderingly, not quite believing he was really there. And then I'd fallen asleep. And when I woke up, he was gone. The stab of disappointment, of loss, had remained with me till this day. It was something I didn't want Jonathan to feel.

As time passed, and still Jonathan didn't wake up, I became hungrier and hungrier. And I was dying to go to the loo. I shouldn't have had that cup of coffee! But I wouldn't leave him. I didn't care if I passed out with hunger, or left a puddle on the floor. I would not leave him.

At long last he opened his eyes and gave me such a pitiful look that I wanted to cry. I stayed until he was fully conscious, and then explained that I was just popping out for a short while to get something to eat. He nodded his understanding, and I made a dash for the nearest loo. Then I fortified myself with a bowl of thick German pea soup and chunks of four-corn bread.

On the way back from the restaurant I lost my bearings, and I stood hesitating in a long corridor, with numerous doors opening off it, and several flights of stairs. A doctor came by and asked if he could help, and I told him I was looking for the Aufwachsraum, thinking this was German for Recovery Room (literally "waking up room"). His mouth twitched as he gave directions, and I wondered what I'd said wrong. When I reached the room and read the sign on the door, I discovered that I should have said the Aufwachraum, and I smiled as I realised that what I had actually asked for was the growing up room.

Jonathan recovered quickly from his ordeal. And, he *was* growing up — as we were. No longer the immature parents we had been with Mark, afraid of what the social workers would think, afraid of him getting injured and our being accused of child abuse, we were learning to stand back and let Jonathan be the judge of what he could and could not do. At times, our hearts were in our mouths, but we knew that if Jonathan was going to become independent, he would have to take risks. And children who take risks sometimes get hurt. We would always be there to help and comfort. But we would never stand in his way.

Jonathan was now trying a new skill: jumping on and off the pavement kerb. One day, as I was chatting to a neighbour and Jonathan was practicing his jumps, she asked, "Aren't you afraid that he will go over on his ankle and break it?"

Of course I was afraid. But I wasn't going to stop Jonathan from jumping, or from running, two things that he still couldn't manage very well, and that made him look very unsteady. Every moment he looked as if he was about to be flung off balance, or trip and go flat on his face.

One day, his ankle did give way. He was running to the car in a sloping car park, and he was thrown sideways, badly grazing his elbow and knee. He was very tired at the time, not having had his afternoon nap, and he screamed the place down. And he continued to howl long after we'd settled him in the car and begun the journey home. "It will soon feel better," I assured him for the umpteenth time. "And I'll put some cream on your elbow and knee when we get home. Then it won't sting so much. There's no need to cry."

The howling stopped abruptly. And in the sudden silence, he said indignantly, "But I want to cry."

Brian and I exchanged smiles. Then I told Jonathan to go ahead and cry if he wanted to. He took me at my word, burst into even louder howls, and kept it up all the way home, stopping only when we pulled into our garage.

I had been brought up with the traditional British "stiff upper lip", and it wasn't until I'd had counselling that I was able to allow myself to cry. Jonathan was being brought up very differently. He was learning that it's normal to get angry and frustrated, to feel sad, hurt or disappointed, and that it's okay to express those feelings — as long as they are expressed constructively. I didn't know how constructive his howls were to my poor eardrums! But I was pleased that Jonathan had grasped in four years what had taken me nearly forty to learn. And in putting his lessons into practice, he was reinforcing mine. We were growing up together.

Besides learning how to handle negative — as well as positive — feelings, Jonathan was also learning how to cope with his disability. When he began to realise that there was something wrong with him, he simply accepted it. And he accepted our assurance that the more he tried to use his right hand and put weight on his right leg, the better they would be. I was still taking him to the physiotherapist, Frau Trepp-Jung, but now only once per week. And after the session with her, Jonathan had group therapy while I relaxed in the café next door with a well-earned cup of coffee and slice of cake. At home, Jonathan had begun to do much of his own physiotherapy, so our main tasks now were to encourage and supervise. Life was getting easier.

And then, our good friends, Angela and John, with their family, returned to Germany. As soon as they had settled in, we made the hour-long journey to their new base. I had very mixed feelings. Naturally we wanted to see them again after all these years, and meet their two youngest, born after they returned to the US, and we were eager for them to meet Jonathan. But I also felt apprehensive, and a little insecure. Jonathan had been legally adopted. There was no way Christine, Angela's stepsister, could take him back. But even so....

Like everyone else, they took to Jonathan immediately. And Angela, as usual, was sensitive to my feelings, asking me if I minded her referring to Jonathan as her nephew. Suddenly, the fear dissipated, and I said honestly that I didn't. I was truly pleased that Jonathan was meeting relatives, even if they were not blood ones. But more than ever we were pleased to see his aunt, uncle and cousins lavishing so much love on him.

Angela and her family had done so much for us. But, as if giving us Jonathan wasn't enough, they asked us if we would like to attend a five-day retreat in the mountains of southern Germany. Being non-Americans, we would not normally be able to attend, but her church had agreed to sponsor us.

We had been to one of these retreats once before, when we first moved to Germany, and it had been wonderful. So we accepted their invitation at once. But it wasn't just that we wanted to again experience meeting new people, trying different food, and enjoying lively singing and thought-provoking talks. With this one, we felt that we were meant to go, although we didn't know why. We half believed that Jonathan would be healed. Or perhaps we would receive some new direction. Maybe we would meet someone who would enable us to get a resident's visa, and we could move to the United States after all.

The retreat was, in many respects, all we had hoped for. The scenery was breathtaking, the conversation stimulating, the food delicious — and certainly interesting — and the meetings enriching. But nothing happened out of the ordinary. Although, maybe it was out of the ordinary the effect Jonathan had on everyone, especially at the children's Vacation Bible School.

We had wondered how he would cope with the twice daily meetings, particularly as he was one of the youngest. But we needn't have worried. He loved every minute of it. And, as at the Child Development Center in Wiesbaden, he soon established himself as the favourite. The leaders told us, on the last day, that Jonathan had been a tremendous blessing to them, partly because of his sunny personality, and partly because he was so interested in everything and joined in every part of their programme so enthusiastically. And they told us that he had been chosen for a special honour.

The theme of the Vacation Bible School was "Soldiers for Jesus", and on the last night it was planned that all the children would come marching in to the adult meeting, and take part in the service. Three little ones had been chosen to lead the troops. Two would be carrying flags — one the American flag and the other a Jesus flag — and the third would be carrying a Bible. The child chosen to carry the Jesus flag was Jonathan.

That evening, pride and joy were written all over his face as he came marching in to the beat of a rousing song, his flag held high, with all the troops following. He was, of course, one of the first to reach the platform. And as the other children continued down the centre aisle then spread out into their allotted places, he kept his flag flying high above his head, while he marched on the spot, every now and then doing a little jump, his own variation to the proceedings. Suddenly, I could picture our son marching off into the future, holding high the symbol of his faith, so that others seeing it could follow and be blessed.

But where was Jonathan's future? He wasn't healed at the retreat. And no one had come forward with some formula that would get us into America. For the first time, we seriously thought about returning to England, and we made some half-hearted enquiries about work there. But nothing materialised.

And then, Brian's father died. He was a lovely man, and we hoped that Jonathan would remember him. But he was only five. And since he had spent all his short life abroad, he had seen his Grandad only during our short six-monthly visits.

Brian went back to England for the funeral, and during the few days he stayed with his mother, Jonathan and I walked several times up the hill to Wehen cemetery and looked at the well-kept graves, the flowers and the statues, while I read the inscriptions (translating into English) and talked to him about death and resurrection. I explained, every time he asked, that they were putting Grandad's body in the ground because he didn't need it any more, since Grandad had gone to live with Jesus in heaven, and now had a lovely new body that would never grow sick or old.

On the day of the funeral, I was awakened early by a terrible sound just outside my bedroom window. In my half-asleep state, I lay there confused and shaking, wondering what on earth was going on. Suddenly, it dawned on me. It was a chain saw. I leapt out of bed and pulled back the curtains. But it was too late. They had cut down the willow that overhung the bedroom side of the balcony.

For twelve years, the willow had been the first thing I'd seen every morning when I opened the curtains. In warm weather, I used to go straight out onto the balcony, as it wasn't overlooked, except by the birds and red squirrels; and Jonathan and I had developed a ritual of saying good morning to the tree. Together, through the seasons, we had enjoyed its changing beauty, and we had shared a sense of wonder at the white pussy willows heralding the spring; the beautiful canopy of green, shading us from the summer sun; the glorious autumn leaves that floated down on the wind and formed a thick carpet on the balcony floor; and the breathtaking loveliness of its snow-laden branches in winter. But now it was gone. And I hadn't even said goodbye.

I was still reeling from the shock of losing my beloved willow when I realised that they were hacking off the arms of the silver birch. I was afraid to look, and I found myself saying over and over, "Oh God, not the birch too," while I sat huddled up on the settee, crying myself silly.

It was the first time Jonathan had ever seen me cry, and he put his little arms around me, saying, "Never mind, Mummy." Then we both cried together.

After a long, long time, I decided that I would have to get Jonathan some breakfast, even if I couldn't eat — and that I couldn't sit in darkness forever. I would have to open the living room curtains and face the devastation. I remembered the day we had moved in, and how I had immediately fallen in love with the willow and the silver birch. And the day when I had said so excitedly to the birch, "I'm going to have a baby!"

I thought also of the many times I had put Jonathan out on the balcony in his Moses basket, and how he had looked up into the birch tree's arching branches, chuckling as her leaves fluttered and rustled in the breeze. Then, taking a deep breath, I pulled back the curtains and forced myself to look. The tree was still there. But all that was left of my beautiful, graceful lady was the trunk and five bleeding stumps, open to the morning sky.

An hour or two later, I made myself take Jonathan out. We went for our usual walk, up through the fields to the forest, then, as we had done all that week, along the forest edge to the village church and cemetery. Again we looked at the tombstones, and again I explained why he wouldn't be seeing his Grandad any more — at least, not while we were here on earth. And again, Jonathan asked countless questions about death and dying.

We were back at the house, and I was starting to prepare a late lunch, when Jonathan said, "Tell me the story about Jesus not dying on the cross."

"But Jesus did die on the cross," I told him. And I launched into the story of the crucifixion.

"Not that story!" he interrupted. "I want the story about when Jesus didn't die on the cross."

"What do you mean, Darling?" I asked, puzzled.

"The story about when Jesus didn't die on the cross," he said peevishly.

I wondered if he meant a story prior to the crucifixion, and I started telling him the one about mothers bringing their children to him, and the disciples wanting to send them away. Jonathan was now crying with frustration. "Not that one!" he shouted. "I want the story about when Jesus *didn't* die on the cross."

I did now what I should have done in the first place: I sent up an SOS prayer. "What does he mean, Lord?" I asked.

The answer came back instantaneously: he means the story of the resurrection.

I looked at Jonathan, wondering. "Do you mean the story about when Jesus rose from the dead?" I asked.

His face flooded with relief. "Yes," he sighed.

And now, I began telling him what he wanted to hear: the story of resurrection, of new life.


Brian returned, and as we mourned, not only his father, but our cut down and sawn off trees, we realised that they symbolised everything we were now feeling about Germany. Since the Berlin Wall had come down and the two Germanys reunited, there was a spirit of change, of unrest, and we felt caught up in it. The Americans were pulling out, and my work with them had ended, so we could no longer get on base to attend the military church where Jonathan had been dedicated. And the British group I belonged to was beginning to break up as people moved away, while the leader, now in her nineties, was talking of retiring. We knew that it was time to leave. It was time to go back to England.

Fifteen years ago, we had come to Germany after losing Mark, because we had wanted to start again. It had been Easter time, the time of resurrection. And now, once again, many of the things we loved were coming to an end.. We needed another resurrection.

# Chapter 14

Having made up our minds to return to England, our main concern was finding work, and Brian now began looking in earnest. He should have found a job easily. He was a highly-qualified and respected design engineer with years of experience; he was a technical illustrator with drawings published by the United Nations and the University of Maryland; he spoke fluent German and had done translating and liaison work for several German, British and American firms. But no one wanted him.

After months of fruitless searching, we decided to just pack up and go. We felt that we couldn't hang around much longer as already Jonathan was missing his first year in an English school. And we were feeling more than ever that we were in a kind of limbo. Brian decided to start his own contract firm, and he began writing to various companies, trying to drum up business. I planned to start a private counselling practice, and began making enquiries about counselling in England.

The immediate question was, where should we live? Brian joked that we could just close our eyes and stick a pin in a map of England. But although we didn't know where we wanted to go, we did have some definite ideas about where we didn't want to go. For a start, we didn't want to return to Brian's home town, and neither did we want to live in a built-up area. We wanted to live in a village, out in the country but near a town where there was the possibility of work, and where houses weren't too expensive. But which town? Which part of the country?

That summer, we went to England for our holiday. First we spent a few days with Brian's mum, and during that time we had a meeting with our bank manager. The bank was our only hope of getting a mortgage. We had been out of the country for fifteen years, and neither of us had jobs to come back to. No building society would have even considered us. But amazingly, the bank did. The mortgage consultant was so impressed with our CVs and, we heard later, took such a liking to Jonathan, that he

146

promptly offered us an 80% mortgage, in principle, depending on the house we chose.

We now spent a week in Norfolk, where Brian had an interview, and a week in the West Country, where we had gone camping in our early married days. The interview was unsuccessful. And although I liked the Broads, Norfolk was too flat for my liking; it was too much of a contrast to the mountains of Germany. But the West Country was as beautiful as we remembered it. And although we had never lived there before, we had the strange feeling that we had come home.

Having decided which county to live in, we went on the mailing list of several estate agents; and when we received details of an old village post office, we knew that this was it. The post office-cum-stores had closed down some years previously, at which time the attractive hamstone building had been split into two separate residences. The part for sale consisted of half the ground floor — the old storage area — with a room that would be ideal for counselling, and the entire upper floor, which was in effect a three bedroom apartment. In Germany we had become used to living on one level, so in many ways the house was perfect, although the price was more than we could really afford.

And now, we dipped into our savings for yet another trip to England. We had just one week to buy a house and find a school for Jonathan. We had been particularly impressed by one school prospectus, and we took Jonathan along to meet the head-master and tour the school. It was a mainstream school, out of our catchment area — if we bought the old post office — and we had not told them that Jonathan was handicapped. We thought this might go against him, and that it would be better if they saw him for themselves and were able to recognise his unique strengths and abilities. So we were a bit anxious, wondering if he would be offered a place.

Jonathan impressed them from the start, asking the head-master about pictures in his office of a fire station, and deducing correctly that the school had recently had a visit from them. I smiled inwardly, thinking of Jonathan's repetition of "Fiemasam" on his third birthday. He was no longer repeating things so much,

147

although there were still times when he went on and on, making the same statement or asking the same question.

In the first classroom we visited, Jonathan immediately left us to look at a model that had taken his interest, and he began chatting to a child standing near it, asking what it was, what it was made of, who had made it.... We doubted that there would be tears on Jonathan's first day at school. At least, not from him.

Afterwards, back in the headmaster's office, we asked Jonathan if he liked the school. He said very emphatically that he did. And so did we. It had a good academic record, the atmosphere was friendly and relaxed, and they were able to help with Jonathan's special needs. So we were delighted when the headmaster offered him a place. That was day one. Tomorrow, day two, we would start looking at houses.

We had already decided that we wanted the old post office, but we looked at several other houses, just to make sure. Jonathan had a great time, endearing himself to the estate agent with his many searching questions about what he did, and why people moved, and how much houses cost. He enjoyed one house in particular. The owners had gone to work leaving six little kittens in the kitchen. They all escaped, and the four of us chased them all over the house, trying to get them back. It took an age because, every time we opened the kitchen door to pop a kitten back in, a previously captured one escaped again. Jonathan giggled so much that, as we drove onto the next house — the old post office — we were all in holiday mood.

As we entered the house, we were struck by the cold. It was like walking into an empty warehouse, and we realised that the present owners didn't make use of downstairs at all. What would be my counselling room was just used for storage. I looked at the utility room beyond, and already my mind was racing with possibilities. We could turn that into a library and computer room. Or maybe I could use it for group therapy. But there was a problem: a strong, sickening smell of oil. I commented on it, and the owner, indicating the old boiler in the corner, conceded, "He be smelly today."

The atmosphere changed about half way up the stairs.

148

Upstairs was lived in. But it still had a sad, neglected air about it. The carpet was shabby, paint was peeling, and the décor was dull and boring. Browns predominated, except in the second bedroom which was painted a lurid yellow. It was only half the size of Jonathan's room in Germany, and we wondered how we would fit in our German furniture. But Jonathan liked it. He liked the view over the village green and church, and he especially liked the idea of turning the adjoining bedroom into a playroom. Brian and I looked at each other and nodded. The house would need a lot of work on it, and there would be a lot of expenditure. That boiler would have to go for a start. But it had potential. I sensed that at one time the house had been loved and happy, and already I was looking forward to restoring it to its former state.

The week before, another buyer had made an as yet unaccepted offer on the house. We offered £1,000 more, but still less than the asking price. The owner said that she would discuss it with her husband, who was away on business. She would let us know in the morning.

That night I hardly slept. The three of us were cramped into a small hotel room, and we were near a busy main road. And what with thinking about the house, the noise of traffic, Brian's snores and Jonathan grinding his teeth, sleep was elusive.

The next morning, feeling overfull after an English breakfast, we went back to the estate agent. He told us, smiling, that the owners had accepted our offer. Suddenly, I felt wide awake. We had found our house. Jonathan had his school. And we still had four days left. There was time to explore, to familiarise ourselves with the area, to get used to hearing English again, acquaint ourselves with the new British coins, revert back to inches and pounds instead of centimetres and kilos. And I could begin to learn, for the first time, to drive on the left.

We returned to Germany full of hope. But, apart from the difficulty of buying a house from abroad, we came up against problems we had never envisaged, and months of hassle and stress such as we had never known before. The estate agent referred to the problems as hiccups. To us, they felt more like major earthquakes. The insurance section of the bank wasn't

149

happy about the flying freehold: part of our property being directly over the old shop, now a separate five-roomed flat. And there was meeting after meeting between our solicitor and the bank's legal department, and various other departments — all in different parts of the country — to discuss the matter. And every time they resolved one problem, somebody found another.

The owners of the old post office, understandably, started to get impatient. They were eager to move, and we were holding up the chain. Nevertheless, they kept agreeing to hold on. But we wondered how much longer *we* could hold on. The tension was becoming unbearable, and we started to wonder if we were doing the right thing. Would Jonathan really be better off in England? Or should we stay where we were and teach him ourselves until he was old enough to start at the German Grundschule? Maybe the German education system wasn't as inflexible as we had been led to believe. And Jonathan did speak a little German. If we lost the old post office, we would have to start all over again, and he would then have missed all of his first year of schooling.

The questions and doubts tormented us. But deep down, we knew that God wanted us to have the old post office, and that he would work it out. So we waited, just as we had waited for Jonathan when God had promised us that, one day, we would have a child of our own.

It had been early summer when we put in an offer for the house. It was now December. The bank consultant was going out of his way to get us the mortgage, and he was as frustrated as we were. But at last he phoned to say that a decision would definitely be made at the next meeting. We would know by Christmas, one way or the other. But Christmas came and went, and we were no further forward. Someone had discovered yet another problem. So there would be yet another meeting.

Brian and I wondered about the hindrances. Some of them were bizarre, and happened too frequently to be coincidental — like the work telephones going down when Brian was expecting an important phone call from the solicitor, or the unexplained, deafening noises that happened only when we were making phone calls about the house. We were starting to feel that God had planned something very special for us at the old post office, and that we were in the midst of a spiritual battle.

And then it was New Year. In spite of all the hassle and uncertainty, we had an inner conviction that this would be the last time we'd go out on the balcony at midnight to watch the fireworks. So this year, Jonathan would join us.

He was groggy with sleep as we pulled his thick snowsuit over his pyjamas, wrapped a scarf around his neck, eased his little feet into thick socks and boots, and struggled, as we always did, to get his stiff fingers into his mittens. But as the cold air outside hit him, and the sky lit up with the whooshing, exploding rockets and cascading stars, he suddenly became fully awake, and his little face was alight with joy and wonder as he excitedly waved one sparkler after another, threatening to set us alight with his exuberance.

That year, our gaze kept shifting from the brilliantly lit sky to our little son, jumping up and down and making dazzling circles with his sparkler. And we thought back to that time five years earlier when we had vowed that, despite the neurologist's prognosis, Jonathan would stand on the balcony and bring in the New Year with us. We felt that we had so much to be thankful for, and we knew that the God who had brought us so far would not fail us now.

January and February came and went. The owners of the old post office were making vague mutterings about pulling out. The headmaster phoned, asking if we still wanted a place for Jonathan. (We did.) And then the bank consultant phoned us. "I have some bad news and some good news," he said. "The bad news is that we have decided not to give you a mortgage for the house you want — not with the flying freehold. The good news is that we will give you a 95% mortgage for the house and the flat next door, if you buy both properties together."

Brian and I were stunned. And that night I lay in bed crying into his shoulder. It was impossible! Even though the flat happened to be up for sale as well, and the owner had already moved out, there was no way we could afford it. And the

151

thought of having to spend the next twenty years paying two mortgages — and when we had no jobs! It was crazy! And we wondered, as we had many years before, what on earth God was playing at.

We had planned to keep a few thousand pounds in reserve to tide us over while Brian established his new business and I acquired a few clients. But now, if we went ahead, we would have to use all of this, plus the money from an endowment policy that we really didn't want to sell, to pay the deposit on the flat. We kept thinking we must be mad to even contemplate returning to England penniless, and buying two properties, especially as we hadn't even seen one of them — except from the outside. It could be falling to pieces for all we knew. There was a kind of madness about the whole thing. But deep down, we felt at peace. God was telling us to go forward. So, not without a great deal of fear and trepidation, we went ahead with the two purchases.

I now began thinking more than ever about my dream of opening a Christian counselling centre. It was now a possibility. Although not immediately. At first we would have to rent out the flat next door. But later.... Already I could see it in my mind's eye: a waiting room, two consulting rooms, a staff room and bathroom. My vision had been too small. I had asked God for a house with one room I could use for counselling. He was giving me an entire five-roomed flat. God was wonderful!

But even now, things did not go smoothly. There was hassle right to the end. It was a Friday, about four weeks before we had planned completion, when our solicitor phoned us to say that the old lady who owned the flat was in hospital, and that she was not expected to survive the weekend. He explained that, if we didn't exchange contracts that afternoon, and she died, there would be a long delay as the property would then belong to the daughter, and we would have to start again. He asked us to send the deposits for both properties electronically, so that he could complete both sales, which had to be done simultaneously.

Brian had already sent a cheque for the two deposits, but now we discovered that it hadn't got through. It was drawn on an off-shore bank, so the solicitor had needed to forward it to the

Isle of Man for clearance. And there it had got caught in a local postal strike, so it was still sitting in a sorting office. Brian promptly rushed into action. But he was five minutes too late: the bank had already closed for the day. We would just have to wait until Monday.

That weekend we prayed our boots off for that old lady. And on the Monday, we heard to our great relief that she was still alive. The money was sent across, and we finally exchanged contracts on both properties. At last, it was over!

When the solicitor phoned to tell us the good news, he said, "Now you can go out and celebrate."

But we didn't feel like celebrating. Not yet. We were both exhausted, and I sat down and cried. The last year in Germany had been terrible. There had been a feeling of ending from the day they cut off the birch tree's branches and chopped down the willow. But we had been unable to move on. Being at home all day, now that I wasn't working, I had found it especially hard. Every day I had looked at the mutilated birch, and at the gap where the willow used to be, and I had been reminded of the picture of Jonathan's brain: of the black emptiness where there should have been healthy brain tissue.

During the past few months, Brian and I had experienced a black emptiness of our own; a blackness so deep that it took a while for us to grasp that it really was over; that the old post office was ours, and that now, we really could move forward.

First we gave notice to the owner of our apartment. And it was then we discovered that, according to German law, we should have given a month's notice for every year we had been there. After twelve years in Wehen we were committed to paying rent, the equivalent of £600 per month, for another year — or until a new tenant was found. We didn't know whether to laugh or cry. It was ludicrous. But in a way, we were past caring. What was another £600 to God? He would provide.

Then Brian handed in his notice at work. He returned home that evening with a huge grin on his face. It reminded me of our first week in Germany, when he had returned from work to say that we had been provided with accommodation for six weeks, the exact time needed before we moved into Sigmund Freud Strasse. This time, he told me that the firm had refused to accept his notice because they didn't want to let him go. They had suggested a three-month trial period to see if he could continue working efficiently from England, just commuting to Germany for a few days every fortnight. Our relief was palpable. The three months would give us some breathing space. Now, we had a definite feeling that God was on the move.

In the final weeks, there was a last meeting with my English friends. They presented me with the customary silver spoon, and we reminisced over the good times we'd had together: the monthly meetings, the outings, the garden parties and Christmas parties, and the annual mincemeat making. From now on, I'd be able to pop down to the local supermarket and buy a jar of mincemeat. But I wondered if I would. Maybe I would go on making my own.

There was also a last visit to my gynaecologist, Frau Dr Helfer, as usual taking Jonathan along. She had continued to take an interest in him, ever since the day we first took Christine to her for an antenatal check-up.

We wrote to the social worker, Frau Klammberg, telling her we were leaving, and enclosing a recent photograph of Jonathan. And we had a last visit to the orthopaedic surgeon. We wanted to say goodbye to Dr Lieb, but we discovered that he was away — just as he had been the week Jonathan was born. So now, with the exception of our German neighbours, whom we would leave till the last day, there was just Frau Trepp-Jung.

Brian and I had made her a video as a farewell gift. It was a compilation from holiday, local and at-home videos, including several Christmases and birthdays, and it showed Jonathan's physical and mental progress from birth to the present. It began with him as a baby, first kicking stiffly on his changing mat, then making odd choking sounds as I fed him. (These sequences were recorded, not very expertly, by a neighbour's grandson.) A year later, he could be seen wriggling on his tummy in our holiday apartment in Titisee, and making his first babbling sound. Then followed scenes of Jonathan giggling as he kept trying to sit up, walking with support at my graduation in Heidelberg, pushing his little horse up and down the living room, making a mess with his first ice lolly in Brittany, and enjoying his first paddle in the sea.

Later he could be seen taking his first independent steps in Denmark, holding a ball for the first time, trying to master a climbing frame, holding precariously onto a swing, and whizzing down a slide. At three, the video showed him chasing pigeons — in Trafalgar Square with his eye patch hanging off — throwing gravel, feeding ducks, picking flowers, "reading" aloud a book held upside down, and pushing his stroller through the forest saying over and over, "Jaja do it."

It finished with him marching down the aisle at Sonthofen with his Jesus flag, and doing odd little jumps on the platform while his troops lined up behind him. It was a video full of love and laughter. God had truly made us to laugh.

During the three months it had taken us to pack up, we had celebrated our last Easter in Germany. There had been no pussy willows this year to remind us that the snow would melt and Spring would come, but the birch was starting to sprout new shoots. It would be many years before she was restored to her former glory, and we would not be there to see it. But we had her babies. A year before, she had dropped three seeds into our flower boxes on the balcony, and they had begun to grow.

On the last day but one, I carefully dug up the seedlings, now about thirty centimetres high, and potted them, ready for their trip to England. We would plant them in our new garden, and they would take root, and grow and develop — as we would; the three of us. It would be hard leaving Germany after fifteen years, but we were looking forward to starting again. We had been through a black time, a time of death and destruction. Then had followed a long period of stagnation, when it had seemed that nothing new and exciting would ever happen again. But once again it was resurrection time. There is always resurrection.

# Chapter 15

Five years have passed. Jonathan has just turned eleven. And only now are we fully experiencing resurrection: we feel that we are at last coming to the end of a series of very dark tunnels. And yet, dark though they have been, they have led us through very fertile and, at times, very beautiful country. God has brought us into a fruitful place.

Jonathan got off to a good start with school. He settled in very quickly, and soon became popular with teachers and peers, and had a troop of little girls wanting to carry his bags, help him with his lunch, and generally mother him. At first he struggled with lessons, and needed a lot of extra help and tuition, especially with writing. He was often unable to finish a project because of the difficulty of getting his thoughts down on paper. He has also had trouble with mathematical concepts, and until recently has trailed along at the bottom of the class with this subject. So, understandably, there have been times when Jonathan hasn't wanted to go to school — especially after Brian started allowing him to use his computer. That was much more fun!

Jonathan loves messing about on the computer, and he often disappears for hours on end, engrossed in testing his knowledge and motor skills with the mouse, and finding out new information. It is partly because of this that he has consistently excelled at class discussions with his thought-provoking questions and comments. But much of his progress has been due to Brian's patience as he has sat with him night after night, making drawings and models to explain things, and demonstrate why and how things work. Jonathan still hasn't grown out of the "Why?" stage and the "What-would-happen-if?" stage. And we hope he never will.

Jonathan has also done well with his physical develop-ment. When he was six, he had an operation to stretch his Achilles tendon, and since then has been able to put his right foot flat on the floor. He now wears a built-up shoe, which makes walking easier and enables him to join in games, playing football and rugby with the other children. He still can't use his right hand, but he can tuck a ball under his right arm and run with it, although his gait remains stiff and jerky. It has been some consolation during the bad times to see him running about, having fun, doing the things that normal children do. And I have often had the feeling that God shares our pleasure, and even joins in the fun. We are more convinced than ever that, if Jonathan ever kicked his ball into heaven, Jesus would kick it back to him.

One Christmas, we bought Jonathan a bike. He enjoyed riding it, but has never quite managed to balance without the stabilisers. But one thing he has been good at is swimming. For two years he was involved in a swimming programme for handicapped children — which brought back memories of my Frankfurt days — and he has won many certificates. We have been so proud of him.

Things have also gone well for Brian and me. His three-month contract was extended, and five years later he is still commuting to Germany. Things really improved after the first six months when the owner of our apartment in Germany found new tenants, having spent that time refurbishing it, and we found tenants for the flat we had ended up buying next door. At that time, I obtained part-time work as a GP-based counsellor and was referred my first private client — having first replaced the smelly boiler.

After two years, my private practice had expanded to such an extent that I took on an assistant counsellor, and converted the adjoining flat into the five-room practice I had visualised in Germany. My dream of counselling adult victims of child abuse, of giving to them the skilled and loving assistance I had received, and facilitating healing and growth, has been realised. Yes, God has certainly brought us into a fruitful place. So why, then, did we periodically feel that we had been plunged into a dark tunnel?

The darkness first began when Jonathan's permanent grin changed into a constant scowl, and his frustrated anger into a nasty aggressiveness. In those early days, we often sat down with him, trying to find out what was wrong. Was he unhappy in England? Was he being bullied? Was there a teacher he didn't like? But the only response we ever got was a sullen silence or a belligerent denial that anything was troubling him. Then, one memorable day when he was just seven, he asked, "Mum, did God make a mistake when he made me?"

I stared at him, horror-struck, and answered spontaneously, "Of course not. God never makes mistakes."

Jonathan's eyes filled with pain, and he said slowly, "So — he did it deliberately."

I felt as if I'd been stabbed. And it was a few moments before I could speak. Then I sat him on my knee and talked to him about good and evil, explaining how evil had come into the world, and how we are all affected by it, directly or indirectly. He listened intently. Then he asked, "Was my mother bad?"

From the beginning, we had told Jonathan the story of his adoption. And we had often talked about Christine, being careful to show her only in a positive light. We had explained that she wasn't very good with babies, and knew that she couldn't look after him properly, but that she had wanted special parents for him who would love him very much. And we had told him how she had travelled right across the world, even though she was frightened of going to a foreign country, so that we could adopt him.

But now, I gently explained that, although Christine wasn't bad, she had been hurt very badly and felt sad all the time, so she hadn't looked after herself properly. And I told him honestly, and with a sense that the timing was right, that the doctors had thought Christine's poor diet and smoking were probably the cause of his cerebral palsy.

The effect was catastrophic. Jonathan began to rage, saying that Christine was bad because she smoked, and that her smoking proved she didn't love him. This was bad enough. But soon he turned his anger on me, demanding to know why I hadn't grown him in *my* tummy. I explained as best I could that I had been trying for a very long time to grow him in my tummy, because I had wanted a baby very much. But, far from helping, this made the situation worse. "If you'd wanted me," he said snarling, "You *would* have grown me in your tummy, not in that other lady's, who smoked."

I then explained, in simple language, that there was something wrong with my inside, and that the special little bag that babies grow in was damaged. "In that case," he said nastily. "*You* must be very bad."

Jonathan was obviously struggling with the concepts of good and evil, and we couldn't help him. He had to work this through on his own. All Brian and I could do was pray, and be there, ready with our love and support, when he turned to us for help. But as the weeks and months passed, and he became increasingly more nasty and aggressive, refusing to speak to us or obey the simplest request, we began to think that we had brought a changeling with us from Germany, and left the real Jonathan behind.

Thankfully, there were good days when we laughed and had fun together, just as we always had. Now that we were back in England and near the coast, we often went to the seaside, and Jonathan loved splashing in the sea, making sandcastles — albeit very unstable ones — flying his kite, playing with his frisbee, and joining in family cricket, although he could only hold the bat one-handed. When he began developing an interest in marine life, we started taking him to our local Sea Life Centre, and on those occasions his curiosity and excitement rubbed off on everyone.

His Auntie Pam now stayed with us more often, and with her especially Jonathan loved looking around National Trust houses and gardens. There he was very much his old self as he confidently approached the staff to ask questions about the paintings or furniture, or the people who had lived there. Pam usually ended up treating us all to West Country cream teas, and Jonathan's behaviour in restaurants was always impeccable; while at school, we were frequently told what a nice polite child he was. Yes, the real Jonathan was still there somewhere: the curious little chatterbox, the Sunshine Boy who lit up the world around him. And during a return visit to Germany, the real Jonathan returned in full force.

In order to continue working in Germany, Brian had to do

a computer course at Rüsselsheim, and since it was the summer holidays, we all decided to go. During the hours Brian was at work, Jonathan and I did all the things we used to do in Wiesbaden: we went shopping, visited museums and art galleries, and played in the park. When Brian returned mid-afternoon, we went for long walks in the forest and visited all our old haunts: Idstein, the Rhine Gorge, Frankfurt, Mainz.... And we looked up many of our old friends, including Frau Trepp-Jung, who was delighted to see us all again.

During the entire three-week visit, Jonathan was a joy and delight, although he did drive me demented as he kept asking what things were called in German, then promptly forgetting, so I had to tell him again — and again — and again.

Then, the day we returned to England, he cried pitifully into his cornflakes, saying that he didn't want to leave. And he howled his head off all the way through Germany until the moment we crossed the border into Belgium. Then he abruptly stopped. He was quiet for the rest of the journey. And soon after our return to England, the changeling was back: we were entering another dark tunnel.

But it was in the darkness that Jonathan began to work out his own answers. And one day, when he was eight, he astounded us with his insight and understanding. We were watching, for the umpteenth time, a favourite video: *The Lion, the Witch, and the Wardrobe.* And as the witch called everything evil to her side, in order to fight against Aslan and the four children, he asked, "Why is the witch calling evil things to her?"

I stared at him, surprised at his question, and said, "Well, if the witch is evil, she will want evil things to fight for her."

Jonathan shook his head, and continued to look puzzled. Then he said slowly, "But if the witch is evil, she will think that evil is good."

My mouth fell open. How many adults, I thought, have even begun to grasp that there is no simple division between good and evil; that the good guys don't always wear white hats and the bad guys black? How many truly understand that the wheat and tares have to grow up together because they are so intertwined, even within one individual, and good sometimes appears as evil and evil as good? And I thought back to the time when the neurologist had said that Jonathan would probably be mentally retarded. Although he was microcephalic, having an abnormally small head, and he struggled at times with his learning, he was intelligent and perceptive. And already he had deep spiritual insight. Like the birch seedlings we had brought with us from Germany and planted in our English garden, Jonathan was growing up.

It had often struck me as funny that in Frankfurt, where I'd had counselling, we lived in Sigmund Freud Strasse. Then in Wehen, meaning "labour pains", we'd had Jonathan. And now we lived in a road that was named after the orchard it once was: a fruitful place, a place of growth and enrichment.

But Jonathan's growth did not come easily. He needed a tremendous amount of time and care, and there were periods when he became almost impossible to handle; when he would turn on me angrily whenever I asked him to do something, and snarl, "Why should I? You're not my real mum."

I used to feel so hurt and shut out. I couldn't get close to him, and I started questioning myself, wondering how I had failed him, where I had gone wrong. But it was after one of these periods that the tunnel came to a sudden end, and there before me was a dazzling vista of sun-kissed fields and mountains. It was as if I'd stepped through a magic mirror, just as I had when Jonathan was seven months old, into a Narnia-like country full of love and light and laughter.

It happened when the three of us were out walking. It had rained for weeks, and the grass was sodden and the paths muddy. Jonathan enjoyed walking, although he soon tired and needed help over rough ground or steep bits. So when we reached a very muddy incline, I automatically held out my hand to him, to help him up. We were almost at the top when his foot slipped, and I braced myself, to hold him steady. The next thing I knew, my feet had shot out from under me and I was whizzing down the bank on my back. My legs zoomed through Jonathan's, sending him flying, and we ended up in a tangled heap at the bottom.

I immediately raised my head to see if he was alright. Then I started to giggle. He was lying on top of me, his woolly hat pushed over his face, grinning from ear to ear. Our eyes met, and that promptly set *him* off. And there we lay, the pair of us, giggling and shaking while Brian, with his usual deadpan expression — which made us giggle more — tried hauling us to our feet. And we giggled, on and off, for the rest of the afternoon.

God knew that I needed that experience. I needed to know that there was still a door into a shared world, where there was no sin and sorrow, a world where the great King reigned and everything was perfect. I needed to know because the tunnel we entered next was the blackest yet.

Jonathan was now almost nine, and for many weeks hardly a day had passed in which he hadn't verbally attacked me, standing scowling as he often did with his hand on his hip. This particular day, Brian was in Germany, and I had been counselling some very distraught clients. I was mentally and emotionally drained, so when Jonathan turned on me, deliberately disobeying a simple request to pick up a game he had thrown across the room because he was losing, I was too tired to argue. I gave him a warning, and when he still refused to obey, I slapped his leg. It was perhaps the ninth or tenth time in his entire life that I had used physical punishment, so I was not expecting his reaction. He looked at me with such hatred that I felt engulfed by it. And then, his voice spitting venom, he snarled, "You are an abuser."

The shock doubled me up; and I gasped. I thought I was going to pass out. Then, as the sharp stab of pain turned to a dull, gnawing hurt, I began to cry. Jonathan looked at me for a moment, then he started to howl. And as his howls filled the room, I was thankful, not for the first time, that the flat next door was now unoccupied: he sounded like he was being murdered. I immediately put my arms around him, but it was a good fifteen minutes before I could pacify him sufficiently for him to speak. When he did, he bawled, "I didn't mean to hurt your feelings."

And now we both cried together, our arms around each other, while I struggled with a pain that was tearing me apart. I was thinking of Mark, of the false allegation of abuse, and the grief and torment of losing him. And I was thinking of all the love and patience that had gone into helping Jonathan with the endless physiotherapy, with his frustrations and anger and confusion; the love that had accepted him just as he was, and believed in him; the love that had conquered fear. I had never, for an instant, been afraid that I would abuse Jonathan.

Later, when he had calmed down, he told me: a teacher at school, in his first year, had told the class that if a parent hit you, that was abuse. I was furious! How dare a teacher put such a thought into a little child's mind! How could she be so careless, letting it be thought that discipline and abuse were the same thing?

At first, I was all for going to the school to complain. But the memories of Mark held me back. I didn't want to stir things up. For the first time in eighteen years, I was afraid of being accused of something I hadn't done. So I kept silent. And Brian and I contented ourselves with explaining to Jonathan how we had discussed different methods of discipline even before he was born, and how and why we had decided that, after the age of about two, we would occasionally use physical punishment if we felt that it would be the most effective, for wilful disobedience. We explained that we wanted him to grow up knowing right from wrong, and to be kind and gentle and good. And that, most of all, we wanted him to have a healthy conscience that would enable him to discipline himself, without being too hard on himself.

This incident was another turning point. From then on, we began again seeing more of the real Jonathan: the little chatterbox who giggled and laughed and asked endless questions. He had now entered a "Who invented....?" stage, which coincided with a newly-developed interest in history — although his sense of chronology, and age, was somewhat lacking. He once asked his dad if Henry VIII had been king when he was a boy. And, having made my day by asking me if I was twenty-two, he promptly spoiled it by asking if I was born during the First or Second World War. But most of his questions now, asked in a tone of curiosity rather than anger, were about adoption.

One day, he asked me if he could see a photograph of his natural mother. During the four days Christine stayed with us, we had asked her for a photograph of herself and the father, and we had taken several of her ourselves. And whenever Jonathan had enquired about her, we had offered to show him the photos. But until now, he had always shrugged and said that he wasn't interested. Now, the three of us sat down together with them.. He gave the photo of his natural father only a fleeting glance. He didn't seem to consider him important. Jonathan had never had any trouble accepting Brian as his real dad, perhaps through not yet fully understanding the part fathers play in conception. He looked with interest at the photos of Christine. Then he asked, "Why does she look so miserable?"

I explained that she didn't like showing her teeth in a smile because they were all black and rotten. He nodded. And that was all. He has never asked to see the photos again. And he has never again said, "You're not my real mum."

With the growing change in Jonathan, there was also a change in me as I regained my belief in myself as a mother; a belief that had been fostered in Germany through the many positive comments we had received from our American and English friends, as well as German neighbours and doctors. I also lost the revived fear of false accusation. And we felt happier about our decision to return to England. We had never really doubted that we'd done the right thing, but we had wondered at times, especially when Jonathan told me what his first memory was: the day we moved from Germany. This had saddened me, although later he had added, "I remember throwing gravel while you sat on a bench and watched me."

The bench, I knew, was one part way up the footpath to the forest in Wehen. I often used to sit there, looking out over the village to the pine-clad hills beyond, while Jonathan made patterns in the gravel and threw handfuls of it into the air. He never tired of watching the tiny stones soar upwards, then billow out and separate as the wind caught them; and he would laugh with joy and wonder as they came pattering down around him, becoming part of the path again.

As Jonathan became more settled in England, becoming merged in English life and culture, not to mention picking up the local accent, we too started to feel that we belonged again. And, as Jonathan started coming to terms with his increasing awareness of his disability, laughingly calling it his "terrible palsy", we too began to accept, at a deeper level, that our son was handicapped — that he couldn't always do what other children could; that he looked stiff and awkward as he mounted the platform for school concerts, and tried to clap and dance and act out mimes; and that on sports days he came last in everything and was applauded merely for finishing. And as Jonathan understood and accepted more what being adopted meant, we also began to fully appreciate that adopting a child is not second best, but a very special honour, with a joy and wonder of its own.

As well as learning things at a new, deeper level, Brian and I were also learning that, sometimes in life, we have to backtrack in order to learn something we didn't quite master the first time round. This happened the day we got the dog. We had told Jonathan that we would get him one when we returned to England, but I had vacillated about it for a long time. My father hadn't liked animals — or people for that matter — and had never allowed me to have a pet. So I wasn't sure how I would cope with one. But one day, when Jonathan was ten, I suddenly decided to take the plunge. And the next Saturday, the three of us set off for our nearest Animal Rescue Centre.

We looked at several dogs. I wanted one that was fairly young, good with children, good looking, and house trained — I had no idea how to set about house training a dog — and, of course, one that Jonathan liked. And that narrowed it down to two. We enquired about them, and the RSPCA lady told us that those two weren't good with other animals, and could be rather boisterous. And she suggested Charlie, whom we hadn't noticed because she was sitting in a dark corner.

She was a very nervous dog, a collie cross, and although she came to me at once, she was shaking. It stirred a memory, but I couldn't think what it was. Jonathan took to her immediately, but Brian and I had reservations. Charlie was too timid, too subservient, although she seemed to have a nice nature, and her big brown eyes had a gentle, intelligent look. She was certainly attractive, and we wondered, because of her elegant, streamlined shape, if she was part whippet. She was pure white, except for her black ears and little pointed face, which had a brown and black patch on either side. We spent about half an hour talking to her and stroking her. Then, after taking her for a walk — or did she take us? — we decided, in spite of her timidity and an undershot jaw, that we would have her.

A few days later, an RSPCA official checked our home. And the following Saturday, we went to collect our new family member. It was so simple. And it struck me as so very different from adopting a child.

During that week, we had decided that the name Charlie didn't suit her, and I unearthed our old book of babies' names and spent hours browsing through it. We wanted a name that sounded similar to Charlie. We didn't want to confuse her, especially as we'd been told that, for reasons unknown, she'd been returned from three adoptive homes in the past two months, and was very unsettled. In the end, we decided on Chloe. It means "a new shoot". And as, at that time, we were beginning to feel that we were coming to the end of our tunnels, that there were new vistas of growth and fruitfulness, the name seemed right.

When we got Chloe home, she sat in a corner, shaking violently, and she flinched if we came near her. Suddenly it dawned on me. It was Mark all over again. But her fear did not trigger anger in me as Mark's had done, there were no flashbacks to my own abusive childhood, and I was able to respond to her very differently: with patience and understanding. I knew then that I had come a lot farther on the road to healing and recovery.

Then we discovered that, although she was eighteen months, Chloe had never been taught obedience. So we had to begin teaching her the most basic commands. But worse was to come. She wasn't housetrained! We would take her for long walks and she would do absolutely nothing until we arrived back at the house. Then she would leave a puddle or mess on the carpet. This too was Mark. I used to sit him on his potty and he would do absolutely nothing until the moment I put him into a clean nappy. I used to get so cross with him. But with Chloe, I never felt angry at her fear or seeming stupidity; although I often wondered if she would ever get the idea. It helped that we were planning to replace the carpets anyway, but soon we felt that our house no longer belonged to us. It stank! And no amount of cleaning and scrubbing could eliminate the smell.

Soon, Chloe became known throughout the village. Brian was out walking her one day when an unknown lady shouted across the road, "Is she piddling outside yet?"

On another occasion, Brian and I were out together with her when a trampish looking man on a bicycle stopped and asked in a lilting Welsh accent, "Is she doing her business outside yet?"

I assumed that Brian knew him, and having answered that she wasn't, we stopped to chat. When the man had cycled off, I asked Brian who he was. "I don't know," he replied. "I thought you knew him." And we looked at each other and giggled.

After three months, I was beginning to despair. Then suddenly, Chloe got the idea of where she was supposed to go, although for several months more she still had the occasional accident, usually when she was excited at my return from an hour or two's counselling. But soon she became the perfect house pet: obedient, affectionate, and very protective.

Now, after a year with us, she no longer backs with terror from people carrying walking sticks, or cowers when strangers stop to stroke her. And we are constantly hearing from the villagers the kinds of comments we used to get in Germany about Jonathan: "You've done wonders with that dog!"; "She's lucky to have you."; "Hasn't she turned into a lovely animal?".

With Chloe, the fruits of love, patience and understanding were less entangled with the tares of anger than they had been with Mark, so the rewards were more akin to those we had reaped in Germany, and were again reaping, with Jonathan.

I thought, when Jonathan began talking, that no one reaps what they sow more than parents of three year olds, as he repeated back our words and expressions, complete with our tone of voice and intonation. But now, as I heard him talking to Chloe,

I decided that the same applied for ten year olds. It was myself I heard, the same words, the same way of saying them: "You daft dog! Do you want a cuddle then? You like having your tummy tickled, don't you?"

I was glad that I had never shouted at Chloe — except once: when she dragged a freshly-baked pie off the kitchen work surface, and it landed upside down in a pool of her urine.

Jonathan was also copying Chloe, sometimes unknowingly, at other times with deliberate intent. The first time it happened I was eating breakfast, when I suddenly became aware of Chloe sitting at my feet, her big brown eyes fixed hopefully on my bacon sandwich. Feeling guilty, I ignored her and carried on eating. When I looked again, there was Jonathan sitting at Chloe's side, in the same position, and with his blue eyes fixed hopefully on my sandwich — or rather, one blue eye. He still hasn't had the operation to correct his squint.

I ruffled both their heads, and told them, laughing, to go away and leave me in peace. Chloe slunk away, her tail between her legs, and Jonathan followed her on his hands and knees. I chuckled, thinking of the hours we had spent teaching him to crawl. Now he was crawling easily, without a second thought. And it was wonderful to watch him playing with Chloe: running, jumping, rolling over, playing chase.... In a way, I felt that I had realised my dream of having a house full of children and animals; a house full of noise and fun and laughter; a house full of love. Jonathan could make as much noise as six children. And with Chloe to add to the pandemonium, the fun and laughter also were back. And the love.

Of course, the love had always been there, underneath, even during the dark times. And Jonathan had always known it was there, as he revealed one day when he was nine. I was sitting on the settee drinking a cup of coffee, and he was lying on the rug reading his *Beano*. As Brian walked past me, he leaned over to kiss me, and Jonathan looked up, saying nonchalantly, "You two are sexy."

Unfortunately, I had just taken another mouthful of coffee, and as I burst out laughing I sprayed it across the room. When I had finished choking, I asked, "Do you know what that means?"

"Of course," he replied. "It means you love each other."

He is right, I thought. We do love each other. And as I looked at Brian's blond hair, now decidedly thinner, I thought back to the day he had asked me to marry him. We were now coming up to our Silver Wedding, and we were planning, for the first time since that trip to Augsburg, when I had been afraid of missing Jonathan's birth, to have a weekend away on our own. Yes, ours is a marriage of love. But without Jonathan, it would have been incomplete.

Jonathan has been an essential part of our story, as we have of his. And now, it is time to tell Jonathan the combined story: of his birth and adoption, and of our journey of discovery of God's love and acceptance. It is time because, once again, we have reached an end.

In a few weeks, Jonathan will go to his junior school for the last time. And Brian and I will attend the last sports day there, and the last school concert. It will be sad for all of us because, on the whole, we have been happy with our choice of school. In different ways, Brian and I are also experiencing endings: in my case, the end of a phase in my counselling career, and in Brian's, the end of work in Germany. We wonder what the future holds. But I am reminded of some lines of T.S. Eliot's:

What we call the beginning is often the end
And to make an end is to make a beginning.
The end is where we start from.

# Epilogue

We decided to complete the ending, and celebrate the beginning, by sitting down together and watching the video we had made for Frau Trepp-Jung. And as we watched again the story of Jonathan unfolding on the screen, and experienced again the love and laughter of those first five years, we didn't know what we enjoyed most: watching the film or watching Jonathan creased up with laughter as he watched himself. His favourite scene was one of him struggling to push his stroller through the forest, and for days afterwards he drove me demented as he said over and over, mimicking his baby voice, "Jaja do it."

Jonathan was also very interested in seeing himself looking around art galleries, and he had a fit of hysterics when we told him about an occasion at Cologne when he was four. We had paused in front of a Van Dyck painting showing Jupiter as a satyr with Antiope, who was reclining in the nude with Jupiter's arm draped across her abdomen. Jonathan had looked at it and asked in a loud voice, "Is that Jesus with tummy ache?"

We never had been able to fully work out his reasoning for that one, but now we asked him for some comments on the paintings we had shown him as a baby, when we had wondered what he would say if he could talk. Our normally verbose son summed up each in one word: Picasso and Miró — "Weird!"; Van Gogh — "Cool!"; and Matisse and Macke — "Frosty!". This, he had previously informed us, was cooler than cool.

Later, I read to him extracts from the book, and he especially liked the bit where he kept turning the TV on when he'd been told not to, and eventually doing it with his right hand, knowing that I would approve of that. The following week, on the way to the seaside, Jonathan kept shaking a half-empty bottle of orange juice. It was very irritating, and I kept telling him to stop. Each time, he stopped for about half a minute, then began shaking it again. In the end, I snapped, "Jonathan! Will you please stop doing that! It's getting on my nerves!"

We heard a snigger. Then, his voice piped up from the back of the car, "I'm doing it with my right hand."

I turned round and gave him a look, and he laughed. "Your face, Mum," he said.

"What about my face?" I asked.

He thought for a moment, then explained, "Well, it's smiling at the top and frowning at the bottom."

My face had that same amused, exasperated look on his last day at junior school. He had been given a special award, presented in front of the entire school, in recognition of his very positive attitude, his enthusiasm, and his determination to try everything. We were talking to his teacher afterwards, who told us that, on being handed the book token, Jonathan had leapt up and punched the air in a gesture of triumph, shouting out, "Yeah!"

I turned to him with the look, and said, "I can see that I'll have to teach you to accept awards more gracefully."

And then I almost giggled as I imagined myself or Brian leaping into the air, in our caps and gowns, when being presented with *our* awards at our graduation ceremonies. And I had to force myself back into the present to keep my face straight.

Jonathan smirked. And on the way home, he asked me what I'd been thinking of. He is getting used to my mind being anywhere but where my body is; and when he sees me grinning to myself, or nodding and making strange faces while I have imaginary conversations, he always wants to know what is going on in my head. And he is always interested in my ideas for new stories or poems. While Brian draws diagrams or makes models to explain how things work, I take him into a world of fantasy and stretch his imagination. Together we are enhancing his creative ability and helping him realise his potential. Jonathan knows this. And he knows too that we are very proud of him.

We were especially proud of his last junior school report. His teacher wrote:

I am full of admiration for Jonathan. Ever since our trip to Greatwood [camp], I became aware that nothing was going to stand in the way of him joining in. He is reasonably quiet in class and very keen to please and do what has been asked of him. Understandably, he can become frustrated at times, at perhaps the speed of his work or the difficulty of a practical task, but he battles on manfully and does not complain. In fact, if anything he hates to be wrong, locking horns with peers who contradict and occasionally showing a quite stubborn streak. [Only occasionally!] There are times in class when I have marvelled at his explanations (most often in science), which leads me to believe that there is more to learn about Jonathan than I can find out in a year. He is also renowned for quite a cheeky sense of humour, which he is careful not to display too often. [He displays it all the time at home!]

The report was a fitting end to Jonathan's years at his first school, and Brian and I felt that it was also a tribute to us: to our years of hard work with Jonathan, teaching him to persevere, and to overcome, in spite of his disability.

These past few weeks, while discussing with Brian ideas and possibilities for his new career, and new directions in counselling for myself, I have been getting Jonathan ready for his new school, a mainstream one but with a special needs department. As I shopped for items of school uniform, comparing prices, checking the quality, wondering about sizes, I was reminded of the time I went shopping for baby clothes, and I found myself thinking, as I often have during the past eleven years, how wonderful it is to be a mother; to feel normal.

And now, I have finished sewing in name tags and shortening the right sleeves of his shirts, rugby jersey and blazer, as his right arm is shorter than the other. His new shoes have been built up. And we have taken photographs of him wearing his new school uniform. On some of them, he is standing beneath the tallest of the birch trees we brought with us from Germany, now six metres high; the offspring of the tree that hung over our balcony in Wehen, and whose branches formed a canopy over him as he lay outside in his Moses basket. We will be having prints of the photographs made for various relatives and friends, including Jonathan's Auntie Pam. We will also send a photo to Liz and her family, who are still in Germany; to my ex-counsellor, Cary, and his wife, who are back in the US; to Daniel's parents, also back in the US and busy with their six children and assorted animals; and of course, to our good friends Angela and John.

Angela told me once that she always makes copies of her photographs to give to Christine, who is now married to an older man — not Jonathan's father — and is happy, although she suffers from the lung disease, emphysema. At the time, I wasn't too happy about Christine having photos. It was during the period when Jonathan was telling me so angrily that I wasn't his real mum. But now I don't mind. I am convinced that Jonathan has known who his real mum is from that day with Christine at the American consulate; the day he gave me his first lop-sided smile. He possibly knew before that.

Since that first lop-sided smile, we have come to realise that our twice-special child — special because he's adopted and because he has special needs — has something else special about him: the gift of spreading happiness. He was born with a bubble of laughter inside him. And that bubble of laughter found an echo in me, and it reverberates throughout our home so that even the dog leaps around with a soppy grin on her face. God has kept his promise. He has made me to laugh. And all who hear will laugh with me.

Also by Jennifer Minney

## Self-Esteem
### The Way of Humility

This thoughtful and inspiring book promotes the development of self-esteem on the basis of one's identity in God, through creation and redemption. This foundation, it explains, is essential for creating a respect for self that is humble and grateful, and that leads to a more responsible and effective stewardship of one's gifts and abilities.

The author, a counsellor with a BA (Hons) in Psychology, and more than twenty years experience of helping people with low self-esteem, draws also on her Bible college, nursing and midwifery training to explore and discuss five aspects of the self: body, soul, spirit, heart and mind. With each, there is a survey of common misconceptions and problems, with guidelines for overcoming them.

This book can be used for personal growth and development, or as a study guide for group discussion. A note version is available for group leaders.

For further information on this and other Silvertree titles, please contact:

Silvertree Publishing (Dept JB)
PO Box 2768
Yeovil
Somerset BA22 8XZ

**Also by Jennifer Minney**

## Song of Creation

*Song of Creation* is a beautifully illustrated collection of poems, grouped according to the seven days of creation, and glorifying God as Creator.

There are poems for every mood and need, poems that are sure to bless as attention is focused on God's amazing love, power and diversity. For example, there is the comforting "Dark Night of the Soul"; the awe-inspiring "What is Sky?"; the uplifting "A Bluebell Wood in May"; the tongue-teasing "Fun Fishes"; and the calming "What is Rest?". There is also a thought-provoking section on current environmental issues — creation in danger — drawing attention to man's responsibility towards creation.

This is an anthology you will want to read again and again, and that will make a perfect gift for that special person in your life.

For further information on this and other Silvertree titles,
please contact:

Silvertree Publishing (Dept JB)
PO Box 2768
Yeovil
Somerset  BA22 8XZ